INCLUSIVE BUILDINGS, PRODUCTS & SERVICES
CHALLENGES IN UNIVERSAL DESIGN

EDITOR **TOM VAVIK**

e **tapir** academic press

© Tapir Academic Press, Trondheim 2009
ISBN   978-82-519-2344-6

Layout: Nina Melleby
Cover Layout: Nina Melleby
Paper: 115 g G-PRINT
Printed and binded by 07 Gruppen as

This book has been published with founding from the Norwegian State Housing Bank, the Norwegian Ministry of the Environment and the Oslo School of Architecture and Design.

Tapir Academic Press publishes textbooks and academic literature for universities and university colleges, as well as for vocational and professional education. We also publish high quality literature of a more general nature. Our main product lines are:

- Textbooks for higher education
- Research and reference literature
- Non-fiction

We only use environmentally certified suppliers.

Tapir Academic Press
NO–7005 Trondheim, Norway
Tel.:   + 47 73 59 32 10
Email: forlag@tapir.no
www.tapirforlag.no

Publishing Editor: lasse.postmyr@tapir.no

The book is dedicated to my daughter Kristin.
Her spirit in life gave strength and inspiration for it.

The editor

CONTENTS

FOREWORD

Human diversity is evident across nations and around the globe. People are different shapes and sizes, speak different languages and dialects of languages, belong to different cultures and socio-economic groups, have different physical and cognitive capabilities, have different experience of using products and services, have different likes and dislikes, and have different priorities and aspirations in life. It is normal to be different.

UNIVERSAL DESIGN IS A RESPONSE TO DIVERSITY

The Population Division of the United Nations predict that by 2050 over 21% of the world population will be 60 years old or older, rising from 10% in 2000. Over the same period they anticipate that the potential support ratio (the number of people of aged 15-64 per person aged 65 or older) will drop from 9 to 4. As a result, independent living goes from being an aspiration to an imperative.

UNIVERSAL DESIGN IS GOOD BUSINESS

As we move into an increasingly technological age things have got rather complex. We can communicate on the move, but greater (or different) skills are required to use a telephone. Such advances lead not only to exclusion, but also to frustration or difficulty in using new products and services. Universal design addresses the underlying issues that lead to exclusion and difficulty, resulting in better solutions for everybody.

UNIVERSAL DESIGN IS SIMPLY BETTER DESIGN

This book seeks to explore the potential of Universal Design to create more inclusive buildings, products and services. It comes at a time when there is growing awareness of the need for Universal Design within the design community, increased interest and activity within the academic community and increased commitment within local and national government to initiate change. I commend it to you as it provides access to the latest thinking on Universal Design to inspire designers, researchers and design commissioners to improve our world.

By John Clarkson
Professor of Engineering Design, University of Cambridge
Director, Cambridge Engineering Design Centre

PREFACE

Universal Design targets the needs of those groups of people in society who are excluded from or marginalized by conventional design practices primarily due to age or disability. It links directly to the desirable concept of the inclusive society, but its importance is increasingly being recognized by governments as a focus for social equality and by business and industry as a tool for commercial growth. Designers can also benefit. Designing in a manner that includes the needs of marginalized users can significantly increase corporate competitiveness and value whilst acting as an innovation trigger for designers to think laterally and invent new solutions that address the needs of groups excluded by mainstream design.

There is much literature that exists in the field of Universal Design that talks about this approach from an ideological or theoretical standpoint. This book aims to take these notions and look at them from a practical position. It populates the space between ideology and practice with different points of view. These include the definition of methodology, performance modelling, outlining of design case studies, development of theory and creating inspirational approaches that go beyond the physical need. Importantly, design education and the business impact of Universal Design are also included.

However, the central idea behind this book is to gather knowledge and experiences about strategies and processes that are based on Universal Design philosophy and principles from three different fields: architecture, product design and information and communication technologies.

Architecture, product design, information design and service design are becoming increasingly integrated. Each discipline engages with the other and cooperation and interaction are becoming essential. One barrier to Universal Design take-up is the separatist approach that each design discipline can take and the way in which they are currently seem as distinct from each other. If we can understand the differences and similarities in how we think and work across the different design professions, it becomes easier to learn from each other and move more quickly towards integrated, user-friendly solutions.

The contents of this book examine a key question: What is meant by a Universal Design strategy and how can these approaches be developed, understood and practised within the different design disciplines? To examine this question, architects, educators, researchers, product designers, those working in professional design organizations and researchers from Information Communication Technology (ICT) were invited to reflect on their own thoughts and practices and to write about the design processes and principles they use to create Universal Design solutions.

The book consists of three main sections that mirror the three main areas of focus: architecture, product design and ICT. It begins with an introductory chapter containing background, a brief overview of the history, a summary of the book and initial conclusions.

The book is aimed at a variety of audiences typically including postgraduate students in design and architecture, designers, architects, engineers and business leaders or managers who are working with Universal Design in some way. We intend these essays to be practical and useful both in an educational context and amongst professionals.

A practising designer has to have theoretical knowledge, a systematic way of working, strong values and a positive attitude, and marry these with practical skills and experience. The overall objective of this book is to make a solid contribution to knowledge transfer and generation about strategies and processes that can help those involved in design to develop their Universal Design offer and innovate. It aims to ensure that the resulting designs will include rather than exclude people. We hope that the methods, principles and techniques described here will create more visibility for the end users and be a step forward in achieving and meeting their needs, demands and rights.

Tom Vavik and Rama Gheerawo

ACKNOWLEDGEMENTS

Firstly, my gratitude goes to the authors for their valuable contributions written in most cases under very busy circumstances and heavy workloads. The book is a product of your hard work and it has been a pleasure creating it with you.

This book has been initiated by the editor. My thanks go to the Norwegian State Housing Bank and the Norwegian Ministry of the Environment (NME) for the funding of this book; in particular to Tone Rønnevig at the National Office of Building Technology and Administration in Oslo and to Olav Bringa at the Program of Action for Universal Design at the NME, who both supported my initiative to realize the book.

Furthermore, I would like to thank John L. Clarkson at Cambridge University, the proofreader Anthea Maybury, Martina Maria Keitsch at the Oslo School of Architecture and Design, Onny Eikhaug at the Norwegian Design Council, Jon Christophersen at SINTEF/Byggforsk in Oslo and last but not least Rama Gheerawo at the Royal College of Art Helen Hamlyn Centre for their valuable advice and support.

I am also grateful to the publisher Tapir Academic Press in Trondheim who gave the idea important initial supporting and subsequent advice throughout the editing process.

My last thanks goes to Nina Melleby. She has with valuable advises from Rachel Troye, worked out the graphic design and the illustrations in a truly excellent manner.

The editor

PART 1 **INTRODUCTION**

Tom Vavik and Rama Gheerawo

TOM VAVIK is Associate Professor at Institute of Industrial Design at The Oslo School of Architecture and Design, where he teaches ergonomics and user-centered design.

Since his Master's degree in physiology from the University of Oslo, Tom has gained 30 years of experience in teaching ergonomics to students in product design as well as interaction design and he has lectured at many universities and organizations in addition to conferences.

Tom has published books and articles and has for four years been jury leader of the Design for All category in the annual Design Award program organized by the Norwegian Design Council.

RAMA GHEERAWO is an Innovation Manager and Research Fellow at the Royal College of Art Helen Hamlyn Centre where he leads a team of creative minds working on 'bleeding-edge' innovation projects for business clients and industrial partners. Work includes a people-centred design approach to technology and the projects result in 'real life' inclusive design case studies. Recent partners have included Toyota, Intel and Nokia.

Rama has wide experience in the creative industry having worked in the automotive, product design, multimedia design and design engineering sectors. He was made a Fellow of the Royal College of Art in 2005 for his work in inclusive design and regularly writes, publishes, lectures and talks on the subject to a variety of audiences including students, academics, designers, industry and government.

THE CHALLENGES IN UNIVERSAL DESIGN

Tom Vavik and Rama Gheerawo

CONTEXT AND BACKGROUND

We all have different capabilities and abilities, and these can be influenced by a number of factors including age, gender, lifestyle, genetic heritage and personal aspiration. However, the designed world around us does not generally take account of this wide diversity. Designers often find it easier to design for themselves, to their own aesthetic values and to their own likes and dislikes, and this often leads to design exclusion (Moggridge, 2001). This exclusion can be primarily based on our ability and this can be divided into three main categories: sensory, cognitive and motor. Sensory capabilities include vision, hearing and touch; cognitive capabilities can be divided into thinking, recognizing, processing and communication; and motor capabilities comprise locomotion, reach, stretch and dexterity (Clarkson et al. 2007). In addition, other aspects such as the surrounding environment can also affect personal ability as the rise in asthma and allergies in reaction to increasing pollution demonstrates. Psycho-social competency and other facets of neuroscience also influence our individual abilities and preferences.

However, our capability does not remain at the same level throughout life. We will all experience disability whether it is temporary, as in a broken arm, or permanent, as part of the natural ageing process. New knowledge and strategies in design are therefore required to improve the quality of life through better usability, independence and access for people with a range of abilities. Central to this is direct understanding of the end users' needs and experiences and the development of systematic ways of working that result in user friendly solutions. Designers need to leave their studios and actually meet the people they are designing for. They have to empathize with their lifestyles, understand the issues important to them, gain insights from what they say and interpret this into new design concepts. This should significantly improve what designers have to offer and better the physical, mental, environmental and emotional aspects of any design.

Universal design is the development of an approach that addresses these concerns. It is design thinking that makes the products, services, communication and built environments we create more usable by a greater number of people with little or no rise in cost. This implies that a design should be usable by all people to the greatest extent possible, regardless of age, ability or circumstance and without the need for adaptation or specialized design. Universal design therefore strives to benefit everyone, not only people with disabilities.

THE BENEFITS OF UNIVERSAL DESIGN

The concepts behind Universal Design are sometimes known by other names in different parts of the world. In the UK, this approach is termed Inclusive Design and within the EU the term Design for All is prevalent. Design for Accessibility is sometimes used in information and communication technology (ICT). These names reflect similar sets of ideals, although different cultural, historical and political factors in different parts of the world have affected the precise way in which these ideals have been interpreted and expressed by designers.

Universal Design will be one of the strongest design trends in the 21st century and there are a number of reasons such as:

• Demographic change due to the dramatic rise in numbers

of older people across the globe, seen in its most radical form in Japan and northern Europe, but also evident in China, India and other developing countries. People are living longer today and life expectancy is increasing. In many countries, the over 65's outnumber the under-25's.

- The increasing number of older people is an untapped market potential. Older people hold most of the financial assets in developed countries despite products and services being marketed to younger age groups (Myerson, 2001).

- An increase in the number of people living with disabilities. There are many reasons for this such as: the multiple minor impairments that come with age; illnesses brought on by environmental and lifestyle changes; and the unexplained rise in conditions such as autism, with medical advances resulting in increased survival rates and the increased visibility of handicapped children.

- Legislation fuelled by the disability rights movement. The rights of older and disabled people are multiplying and there is an increasing number of new laws and regulations that affect different areas of society.

- Understanding users can bring inventiveness to the design process and challenge designers to seek new, creative solutions. Working with end users can bring inspiration to the design process as well as providing rich information for the design brief. This technique of close engagement with select users that is prevalent in Universal Design moves the designer from proposing solutions that are self-generated to working with the user in a space that is relevant and beneficial to both their needs. This way of thinking becomes a source for creativity and innovation.

- Universal Design can open up new markets for business by future-proofing products for new consumer groups. Industry needs to make an early response to the growing number of older consumers and disabled users and one of the most robust and 'upstream' ways of doing this is by re-evaluating the design offer they present. Universal design techniques and methods can engender ways of visualizing new design directions and testing them with potential markets to ensure suitability and take-up.

- The need to develop sustainable approaches through equity and participation. Sustainability has three aspects: environmental, economic and social. All three need to be addressed to form a complete environmental solution. A Universal Design approach is a powerful tool in achieving social sustainability.

Above all, Universal Design is about good design, not manufacturing 'special needs' solutions. Older and disabled people do not want to be seen as victims requiring assistive products and services and will not buy design concepts that are marketed this way. Successful Universal Design concepts that have been sold to the mainstream markets are inclusive of people with varied needs rather than exclusively for them. They enable rather than stigmatize.

"In recent years there has been a shift in attitude, away from treating disabled and older people as special cases requiring special design solutions, and towards integrating them in the mainstream of everyday life through a more inclusive approach to the design of buildings, public spaces and, more recently, products and services. This is important for social equality but is also a significant opportunity for business growth through new products and services." (Coleman, R. 2006)

HUMAN RIGHTS AND MILESTONES

Universal Design, like most socially-centered pieces of thinking, has been politically charged since its inception and remains so today. At its heart is a fundamental human right that has been fought over, argued about, defined and redefined since language first enabled conversation and communication enabled civilization. Freedom and choice, the ideological right of every human being, sit at the centre of this approach and 'the affordance of equal rights, access, goods and services' becomes the typical modern day phrasing that still enshrines this thinking.

War and medical invention have also played a role. Throughout history, wounded soldiers have been left to die on the battlefield and people with disabilities were viewed with suspicion or pity at best and hidden away from society. The two World Wars of the last century changed all that. As global tragedies that affected all of humanity, they produced the largest number of disabled veterans that the world ever knew and the invention of penicillin and advances in surgery meant that they could survive horrific injuries that previously would have killed them. Disability was no longer hidden – the veterans gave it visibility in society.

Two further events in recent history accelerated the founding of disability rights. The first was the Black Civil Rights movement and the second was the Vietnam war. In 1955, when Rosa Parks, an African American lady, refused to give up her seat as dictated by Mississippi law, this sparked the Bus Boycott where African Americans refused to take the bus until the law was changed. The bus companies suffered heavy financial losses and relented. This small victory is often credited as a significant turning point in the struggle for human rights which subsequently developed into a powerful political movement. In 1964, the American Civil Rights Act was signed promising "full and equal enjoyment ... of goods and services". Although aimed at racial discrimination, the Civil Rights Movement provided a blueprint for the Disability Rights struggle that followed.

The Vietnam War and the use of helicopters in war zones as airborne ambulances meant that wounded soldiers were evacuated to field hospitals in record time. Again, medical improvements ensured a higher rate of survival and rehabilitation. The world once again faced disability through large numbers of young veteran soldiers who were outraged at the second class treatment they were receiving. Marches on Washington, large rallies and vocal campaigners such as Ron Kovic brought human rights violation on the basis of ability back into social consciousness.

As well as the political dramas that drove the movement, designers, architects and ergonomists also played a quieter, but no less significant role in shaping Universal Design focus and people-centered design approaches. Henry Dreyfuss, a celebrated industrial designer in the US, promoted the philosophy that design should not just be about style, it should benefit people. He contributed much to ergonomics and human factors and his 'Measure of Man' published in 1960 became a defining book in ergonomics and relating design to people. Five years earlier, in 1955, he wrote an iconic autobiography, itself entitled 'Designing for People'. Selwyn Goldsmith, a British architect, was designing with wheelchair users in mind as early as 1963 when he published extensive ergonomic guidelines on designing buildings to include disabled people. Victor Papanek, an Austrian born industrial designer living in the US, once again challenged the style-led approach prevalent in design through his landmark book of 1971, 'Design for the Real World'. He wrote "design has become the most powerful tool with which man shapes his tools and environments (and, by extension, society and himself)." His approach focused on social and ecological considerations and continues to have resonance today.

MILESTONES FROM THE USA

The term Universal Design was introduced in the United States by the architect Ronald L. Mace. He was the founder of the Centre for Universal Design at North Carolina State University and a protagonist in design for varying capability. In 1985, he explained universal design in an article in Designers West. This is the first documented use of the term. Mace formulated the concept of universal design as "the design of products and environments to be usable by all people, to the greatest extent possible, without the need for adaptation or specialized design". Before that, in the 1970s, the US design-er Patricia Moore had carried out an innovative age-simula-tion experiment by dressing up as an 80 year old woman and travelling across the country (Moore, 1985). She was routinely ignored and abused, and on occasion even attacked. Her ap-proach was ridiculed by designers and social scientists alike for lack of rigour, but has since come to be recognized as a 'pathfinding' approach in creating designer empathy.

As a result of the demands from disability groups, the US Federal Government came up with legislation changes as early as the 1960's. Here follow some of the most important legal regulations (UDEO, 2008):

1968: The Architectural Barriers Act. US Congress passes the first law requiring accessibility for people with disabilities in federal buildings. The Act requires all buildings designed, constructed, altered, or leased with federal funds to be made accessible.

1973: Section 504 of the Rehabilitation Act becomes law. It prohibits discrimination against people with disabilities in programs that receive federal funding. This Act makes it il-legal to discriminate on the basis of disability and applies to federal agencies, public universities, federal contractors, and any other institution or activity receiving federal funds.

1988: The Fair Housing Amendments Act. People with dis-abilities and children are added to the 1968 civil rights law that prohibits racial discrimination in housing. It establishes guidelines for universal design in new multifamily housing.

1990: The Americans with Disabilities Act (ADA). This is the most comprehensive civil rights legislation for people with disabilities. The law establishes that the lack of access to pro-grams, employment and facilities is discrimination, in public

and private settings. Access to places of public accommodation, services, public transportation and telecommunications
is ensured by this law.

1995: Principles of Universal Design. The Center for Universal Design develops the first edition of performance criteria
with a group of US experts.

1996: The Telecommunications Act. The law mandates that
telecommunications services and equipment and customer
premises equipment be "designed, developed, and fabricated
to be accessible to and usable by individuals with disabilities,
if readily achievable." It applies to all types of telecommunications devices and services, from telephones to television
programming to computers.

1997: A group of architects, product designers, engineers and
environmental design researchers works out seven principles
of universal design as a guide for a wide range of design disciplines including environments, products and communications. The principles are broader than those of accessible design and are: 1) Equitable use. 2) Flexibility in use. 3) Simple
and intuitive use. 4) Perceptible information. 5) Tolerance for
error. 6) Low physical effort. 7) Size and space for approach
and use. Each principle is given a definition and guidelines
are worked out (CUD, 2008).

UK AND EU MILESTONES

The UK and EU have followed a path that is based less on
legislation changes and political decisions than the US. Early
milestones were based on rehabilitation needs and design-
led approaches instead. Because of this, disability legislation
post-dates the American equivalents but the UK and EU have
worked hard to catch up. At the time of writing, some European legislation now leads the world.

1948: Sir Ludwig Guttmann, a German neurologist at the

rehabilitation hospital in Stoke Mandeville, England, organizes a sporting competition involving World War II veterans with spinal cord injuries to help with rehabilitation. This becomes the Stoke Mandeville Games held in the same year as the 1948 Olympics in London. Games are held annually.

1952: The Netherlands join the Stoke Mandeville Games creating the first international competition for disabled people.

1960: The 9th Stoke Mandeville Games are held in Italy after the Olympics. This is considered to be the point at which the Paralympics were established.

1963: Architect Selwyn Goldsmith creates building guidelines for people with disabilities.

1968: The International Commission on Technology and Accessibility and Rehabilitation International run a competition to design the International Symbol for Accessibility. An entry by Danish student Susanne Kofoed is accepted in 1969 with minor modifications. A head is added to her iconic blue and white line drawing of a wheelchair user. The symbol is now used internationally.

1976: The United Nations launches its international year for disabled persons.

1979: Ergonomi Design Gruppen is formed in Sweden by a group of designers including John Grieves and Maria Benkzton who believes in a people-centered approach. The group is formed by the merging of two existing companies, Ergonomi founded in 1969 and Design Gruppen in 1971. Their approach is user-orientated and socially inclusive and continues to be a central part of their philosophy today.

1986: The Helen Hamlyn Foundation organizes the New Design For Old exhibition in London, a pathfinding exhibition that challenges leading designers to create design concepts for older people.

1995: The UK Disability Discrimination Act 1995 is passed by parliament making it unlawful to discriminate against people in respect of their disabilities in relation to employment, the provision of goods and services, education and transport. It is a civil rights law as opposed to being a constitutional or criminal law.

1999: The Helen Hamlyn Centre is founded at the Royal College of Art in London, UK to advance the practice of inclusive design, working with students, professional designers, academia and industry. It is one of the few centers in Europe that focuses exclusively on inclusive design.

2000: The UK Department of Trade and Industry, part of the UK government, defines inclusive design as 'a process whereby designers ensure that their products and services address the needs of the widest possible audience'. This is part of their Foresight Programme and presents inclusive design as a potentially important driver of change.

2004 - The UK Disability Discrimination Act is modified as follows: service providers may have to make other 'reasonable adjustments' in relation to the physical features of their premises to overcome physical barriers to access.

2005: BSI British Standards publish a new standard, 'BS7000-6: Guide to managing inclusive design'. It provides a comprehensive framework to help all enterprises, public sector and not-for profit organizations to introduce a professional approach to inclusive design.

2006: The United Nations agrees on the Convention on the Rights of Persons with Disabilities. This is the first human rights treaty of the 21st century, aimed at increasing and upholding the rights of the estimated 650 million disabled people across the world.

SUMMARY OF CONTENTS

The contributions in this book are divided into three sections Architecture, Product Design and Services. Each one is summarized in the following pages.

PART 2. ARCHITECTURE

In his chapter, Paradigm for the 21st century: The challenge for implementing universal design, Preiser refers to The Universal Design Handbook (Preiser and Ostroff 2001). This handbook gives standards and guidelines and "evidences increasing acceptance of and activity in universal design, in Europe and North America, and especially in Japan". He gives us three main strategies for implementing and organizing universal design: A short-term one by carrying out evaluations of existing facilities; a medium-term strategy by carrying out programming projects for future facilities by incorporating universal design criteria from the start, and by integrating them with existing standard building performance criteria; and a long term one by bringing "universal design into curricula of planning and design schools as a required subject matter". Furthermore, Preiser discusses the Seven Principles of Universal Design and argues that they are relative concepts and that the principles "may be perceived differently over time by those who interact with the same environment, facility or building, such as: owners; occupants; management; maintenance personnel; and passersby or visitors". In his contribution he puts emphasis on evaluation based on a consumer feedback-driven and post-occupancy evaluation process. Based on user needs he then presents three levels of building performance criteria and a process model for universal design evaluation (UDE). As a strategy for UDE he concludes with a fusion of performance and universal design criteria "moving from primarily subjective, experience-based evaluations to more objective evaluations".

Christophersen presents in his chapter, Development, Promotion and Execution of Universally Designed Housing in Norway, an overview of the last forty years. He explains two main reasons for the relatively slow progress in this field: the process of "altering the mindset of the general public and the local and central decision makers" and: the involvement of a conservative industry, heavy technology and installations of a permanent nature. As a solution to this challenge he suggests "a simultaneous bottom-up/top-down approach" that gives "opportunities for top level policy-making and for conveying the needs of the users to the industry in a way that makcs it possible to develop cost effective solutions". Christophersen states that "moderately increased levels of usability and accessibility can be achieved at a small and often negligible extra cost". He claims that what is lacking is "an approach towards creating efficient, rational and practicable performance criteria for Universal Design". Without precise performance criteria it will be problematic to put the requirements into practice. Following the 'learning by doing principle' he ends up presenting a series of illustrated examples of universal designed solutions in different projects completed across Norway.

The next author, Asmervik, takes up the pedagogic challenge of universal design in his chapter, Teaching universal design to students of architecture. He claims "that prestigious architecture and architects do not pay enough attention to the needs of users" and he forces students to devote attention to the needs and requirements of different user groups. "Industrial designers are already quite familiar with this way of thinking .... Architects and landscape architects have a strong tradition based on the idea that the individuals' "signature projects" are the real objective of their activity", he writes. As a pedagogic method he goes through seven famous architectural projects around the world and comments on and criticizes the universal design aspects of these. Furthermore, he presents assignments and exercises for students. By outlining tasks and asking questions he puts emphasis on solutions, attitudes, strategies and processes

15

concerning universal design when applied to the field of architecture.

In the last chapter in part 1, Architecture for the Senses, Ryhl takes as a starting point the concept of accessibility. In the context of architecture accessibility traditionally means accommodating physical disabilities and generally ensures everyone of physical access to a given space. She introduces a new design concept: sensory accessibility as a parallel and complement to existing concepts. Sensory accessibility "ensures that everyone can stay in the space and be able to participate, enjoy and experience". Her research is based on interviews and 1:1 testing in existing housing with people living with a sensory disability. Ryhl describes and explains the importance of designing for all of our five senses - vision, hearing, touch, smell and the kinesthetic sense of balance. Within each of these categories she gives valuable advice and guidelines as to how to create good architecture that is highly appealing. The conclusion is that the end user should experience sensory accessibility in addition to physical accessibility.

PART 3. PRODUCT DESIGN

In his chapter, Designing a more Inclusive World, Clarkson introduces the basic elements of good business practice. His emphasis is on "understanding the real user and business needs at the start of the design process and correctly translating these needs into an appropriate requirements specification". To demonstrate the potency of this approach, he points out several successful design companies that have followed this strategy.

He then gives us the drivers behind Inclusive Design: the importance of independent living for an ageing population and the fact that our capability varies continuously throughout life. "Inclusive design places the responsibility with product designers to ensure that the capability levels required to use a product are as low as possible". Clarkson presents a "waterfall" model for an inclusive design process in four steps: discover, translate, create and develop. To understand and measure user capabilities, seven capabilities are described and categorised.

The next section of his chapter provides some examples of user capability loss and the challenges these might pose to effective use of products and services. Sensory, cognitive and motion capability losses are described and examples of problems in daily life are given.

To counteract these problems Clarkson emphases the following approach: involving the user in the design process and using design tools such as physical and software simulators. "A particularly effective approach is to combine the use of user trials, expert assessment and exclusion audits to review a new product".

The next author, Eikhaug, argues in her chapter, Design for All, a commercial perspective, that product development processes based on Design for All principles are a strategic tool for innovation and business development. She claims that one of the challenges for companies and businesses is to have a wider perspective when considering design. Aesthetic, functional or emotional needs are not enough. "Attention has to be focused on the role design can play in promoting sustainability, enabling human rights and creating social inclusion." Eikhaug states that a Design for All approach helps "to identify new potential products, services or innovations and thereby capture a larger market with inclusive solutions".

Regarding legislation, in all markets, both nationally and internationally, a "more stringent legislation is being introduced to support Design for All and accessibility". This new legislation involves challenges but can also be seen as bringing "opportunities for innovations and creating competitive advantages".

As a strategy for better design she emphasizes a user–centered design process and presents three case studies based on this. Eikhaug points out new trends in inclusive marketing and advertising and ends her chapter with four criteria to introduce a Design for All strategy into a company's core practice.

Rønneberg Næss and Øritsland, in their chapter Inclusive, mainstream products, ask the question "Do people want to use inclusive products?". Their issue is not usability and utility but the emotions and values that people connect with when using products. They look at how to achieve dignity and enjoyment and how to create an attractive identity when designing assistive products. A strategy based on communication theory is presented and they "propose that affordances, denotations and connotations may be applied as levels of analysis and ideation". The authors quantify and describe the kind of meaning generated at each of the three levels as follows:

> *Affordances before meaning* – what is it possible to use it for?
>
> *Denotative meaning* of product – what is it, what do you do with it?
>
> *Connotative meaning* of product – what does this product say about you in different social contexts? How will your using it be interpreted?"

"By analysing activities and products at these three levels, a creative process can explore alternative or supplementary product functions and principle structures", they argue. In the last part of the chapter they explain their theory through practical examples and suggest two approaches for inclusive design. The first is an approach that secretly and discreetly adapts mainstream products and the second is a styling approach where desirable values and features are added to assistive products.

In the chapter The Small Design Changes that Make a Big Difference – a Case study in Packaging Design from the

Norwegian Company Jordan, Støren Berg presents a well
documented and illustrated study where she describes a
concrete and practical example of a design for all approach in
seven steps. The strategy consists of three main elements: "1)
involving users with disabilities as lead users, 2) providing a
tool for design decisions accounting for all aspects of design,
and 3) a workshop procedure to integrate the Design for All
approach with the existing project process at the company".
Users with arthritis, visually impaired users, older people,
children and users without capability loss were invited into
the design process at different stages. A design for all criteria
tool was developed and used "to create a common understanding and common language for the user experience
aspects of the packaging". Støren Berg states that "it was possible to improve the packaging in the most critical area, even
with the tight constraints of technology, logistics, unit cost,
and contradictory design requirements". One of the experiences from this project is that a Design for All approach is
about "balancing, compromising and bridging conflicting
requirements".

PART 4. SERVICES

Skeide Fuglerud presents in her chapter, Universal design in
ICT services, "arguments for universal design in information
and communication technology (ICT) services and discusses
the importance of integrating universal design activities
into the development process". She describes the difference
between ICT products and ICT services and states that "an
ICT service involves a service provider each time it is used"
and that services "often have both internal users (working
for the service provider) and external users (other service
providers and customers)". She argues that developing ICT
services involves many stakeholders and considerations and
that universal design activities should be integrated into the
overall project's life cycle as well as the software development
process.

An internationally important policy goal is referred to as

e-inclusion and to achieve this products and services have to be designed to be accessible to as broad a range of people as possible. This includes also people placed in "impairing environments". Furthermore, she argues that the trend in the western world towards e-Government and towards a self-service society will escalate the challenges concerning accessibility and disabling conditions. On the other hand she claims that "the possibilities of making universally designed ICT solutions have never been better" and she gives us arguments for her view. Multimodal interaction is one strategy. "There is a fundamental connection between multimodal interface design and universal accessibility", she argues. A list of examples where users in constraining situations or contexts and impaired users may produce the same or similar requirements for a system is presented. In the last half of her chapter Skeide Fuglerud gives us instructions and advice on how to incorporate a universal design approach into a design process, based on her own experience. It is crucial for success to have "commitment and support from the service or project owner, the management and personal commitment and individual leadership".

Someone in the design team must therefore have the responsibility, the mandate and authority for the universal design focus in the project, she argues. In the design process you have to "plan for iterations, user involvement and changing requirements". "Tasks and users are equally important" is her experience. "You have to do a thorough job of end user research" and "based on personas one can create different scenarios and narratives as a starting point in the design process". In the evaluation process use of accessibility tools, heuristic evaluation and user tests is recommended.

In his chapter, Design for All in ICT, Mellors presents a three level model for adopting the Design for All approach when designing Information and Communications Technology (ICT) products. On the base level he puts mainstream designed products for all that can be used by a broad range of users. The next level he describes as products "providing connection for assistive devices". The top level of the model consists of one-off, specially designed products for very disabled users. Furthermore he argues that the ISO/IEC Guide 71 is a valuable introduction for identifying abilities and disabilities among users "to have direct impact on the successful use of ICT products and services". To follow up legal regulations in this field he recommends ISO/IEC 13407: Human-centered design processes for interactive systems and ETSI EG 202 116: Human Factors; Guidelines for ICT products and services "Design for All". Mellors claims that Design for All must in practice remain Design for Most. Moreover, he states that two complementary approaches are needed to enable disabled and elderly people to lead full and independent lives; the Design for All approach and the Assistive Technology (AT) approach. In the last part of the chapter, he goes into how "to enable an assistive device to be used in conjunction with other ICT equipment". Mellors ends up with a description of technical solutions and examples of how information can be exchanged with assistive devices and services. He concludes that "for assistive devices to become affordable and effective, the significant players in each field need to agree on a set of protocols to be used in the communication between assistive devices and relevant ICT devices".

Hestnes, Brooks & Heiestad describe the proposal and testing of a communication service concept that assists blind and visually impaired people. In the paper Use of Mobile Video telephony by Blind People: Increasing independence and spontaneity for day-to-day life, they write that "videotelephony for blind persons may sound like a contradiction in terms". "However, using two-way audio and one-way video from a blind or visually impaired person to a service operator, a new and important communication service may have been born", they claim. The operators act as guides and with the videophone the visually impaired persons can "obtain information" from their surroundings.

The authors conducted focus group studies "to identify initial user and technical requirements", longitudinal observation "studies of leisure- and business use to identify specific needs", "user tests performed on five identified situations", "tests on technical quality reduction" and field trials with 3G mobile handsets. They classified three main situations when the video call was used: "To verify information or objects when found", "to search for information or objects" and "to observe a situation, object or environment". The five most relevant situations identified and tested were: "Mini-bank; Shopping; At a bus stop; Finding something lost on the ground and Being lost". The visually impaired participants were interviewed and the following main communication goals were expressed: Greater freedom and independence; Spontaneity; Improved safety and Efficiency. 6 of 9 participants answered yes to the question whether a mobile call service had helped make their lives simpler. The test results where used "to develope guidelines for industry on user quality of experience".

CONCLUSIONS

The contributions in this book look at theory, methodology and practice in Universal Design from different angles. Although divided according to the different design disciplines of Architecture, Product Design and ICT Services, they importantly bring voices from business, education and design consultancy into the discussion. These are important communities to include as the success of Universal Design relies on moving it forward from ideology towards practice, and demonstrating its relevance to each of these communities becomes critical in enabling this.

However disparate the backgrounds of the authors in this book, a common theme in all their work is the championing of user engagement and the relevance of a people-centred design approach. This is the central premise of Universal Design. Designers have to get out of their studios and design for the real world around them. Working closely with users encourages empathic bonding between designer and user, creating a space where they can both act as equals to address the problem in hand. Bonding with the user helps the designer understand lifestyle and aspirational factors that are all too often overlooked, moving beyond ergonomic problem solving into an area of creative thinking and user-facilitated innovation.

Benefits of a Universal Design approach go beyond moral principles or a doctrine of social betterment. It is also about bettering design, improving business and attracting under served consumer groups. Understanding users can bring inventiveness to the design process and open up new markets for business by future-proofing products for new consumer groups. Industry needs to make an early response to the growing number of older and disabled consumers and one of the most robust and 'upstream' ways of doing this is by re-evaluating the design offer they currently present. Universal Design techniques and methods can engender ways of visualizing new design directions and testing them in potential markets to ensure suitability and take-up.

Universal Design will become increasingly important in the future. It is one of the strongest trends in design and it is happening now. It is directly engaged with the concept of social sustainability and inclusion, ideas that have growing importance in the political arena and in the corporate world. Most importantly it can also act as a catalyst for designers to innovate and as a framework for inspired creation. It is hoped that these pages will contribute to the history and practice of Universal Design and play a role in envisioning a brighter future.

REFERENCES

Clarkson et al., 2007. Inclusive Design Toolkit. Cambridge: Engineering Design Centre, Department of Engineering, University of Cambridge.

Coleman, R., 2006. An introduction to inclusive design. Design council. 10 Nov. 2006 . Updated 26 April 2007. Available at: http://www.designcouncil.org.uk/en/About-Design/Design-Techniques/Inclusive-design/. Accessed 31 Oct. 2007.

CUD, the Center for Universal Design. Available at: http://design.ncsu.edu/cud/index.htm Accessed 19 June 2008.

Moore, P., 1985. "Disguised: A true story". Word Books, Waco, Texas, USA. ISBN 0-8499-0516-8

Moggridge, B., 2001. "i Magazine: Magazine for the Design Council, issue 6". The UK Design Council, UK, pp 12-13

Myerson, J., 2001. "Design DK: Inclusive Design". (Reprint) Danish Design Centre, Denmark, p 5.

UDEO, Universal Design Education Online. Available at: http://www.udeducation.org/resources/readings/mueller_mace.asp Accessed 19 June 2008.

PART 2 **ARCHITECTURE**

Wolfgang F. E. Preiser
Jon Christophersen
Sigmund Asmervik
Camilla Ryhl

WOLFGANG F. E. PREISER is Professor Emeritus of Architecture with the University of Cincinnati, USA. On a global level, he has lectured at 109 universities and organizations, in addition to many conferences. As a researcher and international building consultant, he has worked on topics ranging from universal design to facility programming, building performance assessments, health care facilities, and intercultural design in general. He is widely published, with 15 books and 125 chapters, articles and papers in conference proceedings to his credit, and he serves on the editorial boards of major journals. Preiser has received many honors, awards and fellowships, including the progressive architecture applied research award and citation, professional fellowships from the national endowment for the arts, the edra career award, and the fulbright fellowship.

PARADIGM FOR THE 21st CENTURY: THE CHALLENGE OF IMPLEMENTING UNIVERSAL DESIGN

Wolfgang F. E. Preiser

INTRODUCTION

Various definitions for universal design have been offered, including that by the Center for Universal Design (Story, 2001). The meaning of "universal" in this context is to make products and environments usable by a majority of people, regardless of gender, disability and health, ethnicity and race, size, or other characteristics (Mace, Hardie and Place, 1991).

Could it be that "universal design" is an oxymoron? Stephen Kurtz (1976) observed in "Nothing Works Best:" " . . . the designer is faced with a multitude of groups, often conflicting, who do not share common educational or class values, and who have little experience in major decision making."

Previous attempts at designing environments for all to use did not necessarily meet with success: the Usonian house, designed by Frank Lloyd Wright in the 1950s, was to make affordable housing accessible to everybody. As it turned out, it was not very affordable and barely habitable, with the kitchen and bedrooms the size of closets.

What features should a universally designed car or house have in an age where mass-produced goods can be customized by literally thousands of choices? On one hand, current car production techniques demonstrate that the consumer is king and the same production line can assemble cars with seemingly limitless variations. Feedback, feed forward and control are the watchwords (Preiser, 2001) in a world of

changing paradigms (Petzinger, 1999) in which information and knowledge is the new currency (Figure 1). Dee Hock
(2005), and more recently John Naisbitt (2006) are among
those who are challenging traditional paradigms of how the
world works, and how to manage an accelerating and constantly changing dynamic at the individual, organizational/
community and global levels.

PARADIGMS LOST...AND GAINED
TWO BUSINESS WORLD VIEWS AND WHAT THEY MEAN

MECHANICAL MODEL	NATURAL MODEL

SCIENTIFIC LEADERS

Newton	Einstein
Galileo	Quantum Physicists
Descartes	Chaos, complexity theorists

CENTRAL METAPHORS

| Machines | Organisms |
| Clocks | Ecologies |

STRATEGIC OBJECTIVES

Optimum design	Adaptation
Consistency	Continuous
of operation	improvement

CULTURAL EXPRESSIONS

Classical music	Blues and jazz
Renaissance	Postmodern art
painting	

LEADERSHIP IMPLICATIONS

Command and	Autonomy for
control	employees
	Articulation of vision

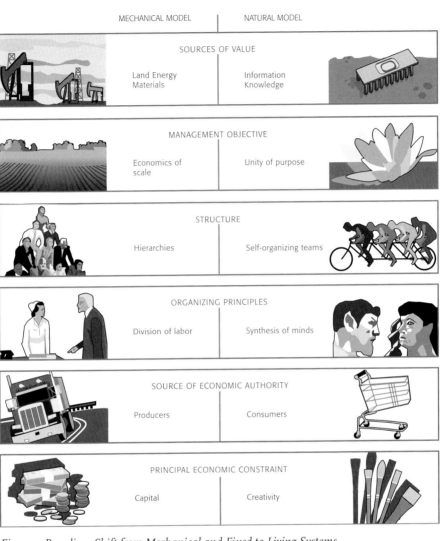

Figure 1: Paradigm Shift from Mechanical and Fixed to Living Systems

On the other hand, in the U.S. housing market banks dictate the features and sizes a house must have in order to be resalable, individual choices and variations are minimized, and the "cookie cutter" approach to housing design is pervasive. The result is that only a tiny minority of houses are designed by architects, and almost none are accessible from a universal design perspective.

UNIVERSAL DESIGN

How universal is universal? In a homogeneous community and culture it is possible to define and describe cultural norms and expectations, as far as products, spaces and buildings are concerned. However, in a world which is getting ever more diverse and globalized, the question has to be asked whether any one standard or set of criteria can universally meet everybody's expectations and needs.

Serious issues of relativity and establishing priorities in universal design arise when dealing with different cultural contexts. Not only do space, lighting and other standards vary considerably across cultures for the same types of environments, such as housing or offices, but economic conditions, technological developments, and culture-specific customs and patterns of space utilization add to the complexity of this question.

IMPLEMENTING UNIVERSAL DESIGN

The Seven Principles of Universal Design, as developed by the Center for Universal Design (1997), constitute ideals which need to be operationalized for use in the real world, and in everyday design situations. Some products, such as "Mr. Good Grips" kitchen utensils by OXO and Fiskars scissors, have been developed to meet universal design needs. Much less has been done to accomplish this goal in everyday environments, such as homes, offices, schools, transportation facilities, and so on. Despite the fact that universally designed homes are available (Young and Pace, 2001), there is continuing resistance in the design professions and the building industry to adopting the new paradigm. On the other hand, the magazine Ultimate Home Design (Preiser 2006) tries to reach out to these professions by promoting the incorporation of universal design criteria in home design. At the beginning of the 21st Century, there is hope that more universally accessible homes will be built as the baby boomer generation starts to retire.

While there are a number of building types and case studies in the Universal Design Handbook which can serve as examples to be emulated, the only realistic hope of seeing universal design criteria operationalized and implemented is through three strategies:

1. Short-term: carry out evaluations of existing facilities, using the Universal Design Evaluation (UDE) process model outlined below;

2. Medium-term: carry out programming projects for future facilities by incorporating universal design criteria from the start, and by integrating them with existing standard building performance criteria;

3. Long-term: universal design education – infuse universal design into curricula of planning and design schools as a required subject matter, in hopes that, ultimately, professionals will practice what they have been taught about universal design.

UNIVERSAL DESIGN PERFORMANCE

The goal of universal design is to achieve universal design performance of designed products, buildings, and environments, especially at the urban scale. A philosophical base and a set of objectives are the Seven Principles of Universal Design referred to above, with these characteristics in mind:

- They define the degree of fit between individuals or groups and their environments, both natural and built.

- They refer to the attributes of products or environments that are perceived to support or impede human activity.

- They imply the objective of minimizing adverse effects of environments on their users, such as discomfort, stress, distraction, inefficiency, and sickness, as well as injury and death caused by accidents, radiation, toxic substances, and so forth.

- They constitute not absolute but relative concepts, sub-ject to different interpretations in different cultures and economies, as well as temporal and social contexts. Thus, they may be perceived differently over time by those who interact with the same environment, facility or building, such as: owners; occupants; management; maintenance personnel; and passersby or visitors.

The conceptual framework of universal design evaluation is based on consumer feedback-driven evolving evaluation process models developed by the author; i.e., Post-Occupancy Evaluation, or POE (Preiser, Rabinowitz and White, 1988), and Building Performance Evaluation, or BPE (Preiser and Schramm, 1997). The nature of basic feedback systems was discussed by von Foerster (1985): the evaluator makes comparisons between the outcomes (O), which are actually sensed or experienced, the expressed goals (G), and expected performance criteria (C), which are usually documented in the functional program and made explicit through perform-ance specifications. Von Foerster observed that " ... cybernet-ic systems require a motor interpretation of a sensory signal" and, further, "the intellectual revolution brought about by cy-bernetics was essentially a motoric power system or a sensor that can 'see' what the machine or organism is doing, and, if necessary, initiate corrections of its actions when going astray." For example, cruise missiles can read the terrain they are flying over and compare the data with pre-programmed images that are expected, and subsequently, the course will be corrected in the attempt to reach the intended target. The evolutionary feedback process in building delivery is shown in Figure 2. The motor driving such a system is the programmer, designer, or evaluator who is charged with the responsibility of ensuring that buildings meet state-of-the-art performance criteria (Preiser, 1991).

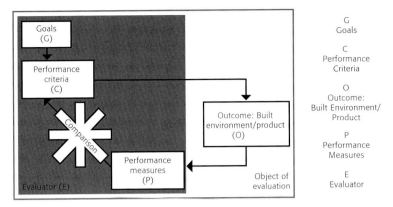

Figure 2: Performance Evaluation Framework (Preiser 2003)

The environmental design and building delivery process is goal oriented. It can be represented by a basic system model with the ultimate goal of achieving universal design performance criteria. It has the following characteristics and elements:

- The universal design performance framework conceptually links the overall client goals (G), namely those of achieving a programmed type and level of environmental quality, with the elements in the system that are described in the following items.

- Performance evaluation criteria (C) are derived from the client's goals (G), zoning, standards, and state-of-the-art criteria for a building type. Universal design performance is tested or evaluated against these criteria by comparing them with the actual measured and perceived performance (P).

- The evaluator (E) moves the system and refers to such activities as planning, programming, designing, constructing, activating, occupying, and evaluating an environment, building or space.

- The outcome (O) represents the objective, physically measurable characteristics of the environment or building under evaluation; e.g., its physical dimensions, lighting levels, and thermal performance. By definition, all elements inside the box (G, C, E, and P) are relativistic and subject to change over time.

- The actual performance (P) refers to the performance as observed, measured and perceived by those occupying or assessing an environment, including the subjective responses of occupants, and objective measures of the environment.

PERFORMANCE LEVELS

Building performance can be structured into three levels pertaining to user needs, as outlined below. With reference to these levels, goals might include safety; adequate space and spatial relationships of functionally related areas; privacy; sensory stimulation; or aesthetic appeal. For a number of subgoals, performance levels may interact and also conflict with each other, requiring resolution.

Framework elements include products-settings-buildings-environments, building occupants, and their needs. The physical environment is dealt with on a setting-by-setting basis. Framework elements are considered in groupings from smaller to larger scales or numbers, or from lower to higher levels of abstraction, respectively.

For each setting and occupant group, respective performance levels of pertinent sensory environments and quality performance criteria are required; e.g., for the acoustic, luminous, gustatory, olfactory, visual, tactile, thermal, and gravitational environments. Also relevant is the effect of radiation on the health and well-being of people, from both short- and long-term perspectives, although many types of radiation cannot be sensed by humans.

As indicated above, occupant needs vis-à-vis the built environment are construed as performance levels. Grossly analogous to the human needs hierarchy (Maslow, 1948) of self-actualization, love, esteem, safety, and physiological needs, a three-level breakdown of performance levels reflects occupant needs in the physical environment. This breakdown also parallels three basic levels of performance requirements for buildings (i.e., firmness, commodity, delight), which the Roman architect Vitruvius (1960) pronounced over 2,000 years ago.

The above historic constructs, which order occupant needs into hierarchies of priorities, were transformed and synthesized into the Habitability Framework (Preiser, 1983) by devising these three levels of priority with nine performance elements:

Level 1 Health, safety, and security performance;

Level 2 Functional, efficiency, and work flow performance;

Level 3 Psychological/social, cultural, and aesthetic performance.

The three performance levels correlate with codes, standards and guidelines designers can use. Level 1 pertains to building codes and life safety standards that projects must comply with. Level 2 refers to the state-of-the-art knowledge about products, building types, and so forth, exemplified by agency-specific design guides or reference works, such as *Time-Saver Standards: Architectural Design Data* (Watson, et al., 1997). Level 3 pertains to research-based design guidelines, which are less codified, but nevertheless of importance for building designers and occupants alike. They are the result of more than 35 years of research in environmental psychology and environment/behavior studies, as exemplified by publications like: *Research Design Connections; Environment & Behavior; the Journal of Environmental Psychology; the Journal of Architectural and Planning Research;* and textbooks on *Environmental Psychology* (Gifford 2007).

The relationships and correspondence between the Habitability Framework and the Seven Principles of Universal Design devised by the Center for Universal Design (1997) are shown in Figures 3 and 4.

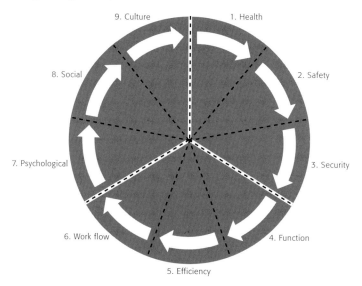

Figure 3: Evolving Performance Criteria

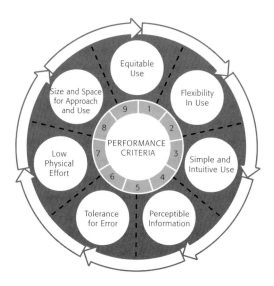

Figure 4: Universal Design versus Performance Criteria

In summary, the framework presented here systematically relates buildings and settings to building occupants or product users and their respective needs vis-à-vis the product or the environment. It represents a conceptual, process-oriented approach that accommodates relational concepts to applications in any type of building or environment. This framework can be used to permit stepwise handling of information concerning person-environment relationships referred to above.

UNIVERSAL DESIGN EVALUATION (UDE): A PROCESS MODEL

The book Building Evaluation Techniques (Baird, et al., 1996) showcased a variety of building evaluation techniques, many of which would lend themselves to adaptation for purposes of UDE. In that same volume, this author (Preiser, 1996) presented a chapter on a three-day POE Figure 5 training workshop and prototype testing after one year of occupancy, which involved both the facility planners/designers, facility managers, and the building occupants. This is a formula that has proven to be very effective in generating useful performance feedback data, a system which later evolved into the Building Performance Evaluation Process Model Figure 6. Merging that process model with universal design resulted in the proposed UDE process model shown in Figure 7.

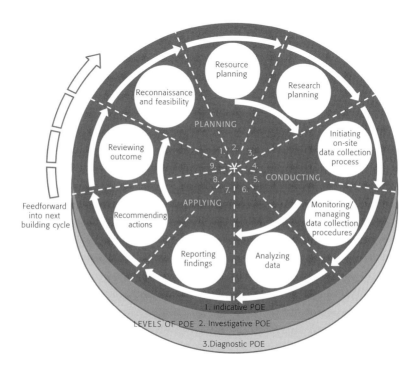

Figure 5: Post-Occupancy Evaluation Process Model

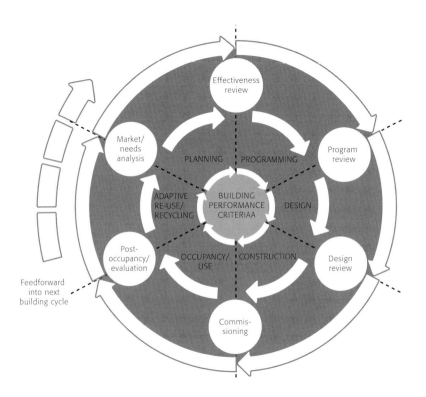

Figure 6: Building Performance Evaluation Process Model

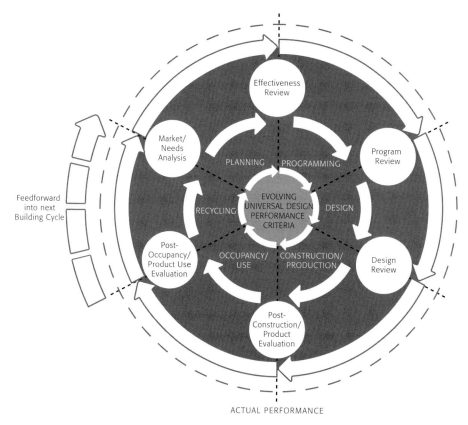

Universal Design Evaluation (UDE): Process Model with Evolving Performance Criteria

Figure 7: Universal Design Evaluation Process Model

Major benefits and uses of the universal design process model include the following:

- Identify problems and develop universal design solutions.

- Learn about the impact of practice on universal design and on building occupants in general.

- Develop guidelines for enhanced universal design concepts and features in products, buildings, urban infrastructure, and information technology.

- Create greater awareness in the public of successes and failures in universal design.

- Establish data bases/ information clearinghouses for proven and successful universal design exemplars, to be emulated and improved upon in future iterations of product and building delivery and life cycles.

It is critical to formalize and document the expected performance of products and facilities in terms of universal design in the form of qualitative criteria, as well as quantitative guidelines and standards.

STRATEGIES FOR UNIVERSAL DESIGN EVALUATION

It is customary to include the Americans with Disabilities Act (ADA) standards for accessible design as part of a routine evaluation of facilities. The ADA standards provide information on compliance with minimum and prescriptive technical standards, but they say nothing about performance – how the building or setting actually works for users with a range of capabilities or disabilities. According to Story (2001), the Seven Principles of Universal Design constitute an occupant need-oriented set of performance criteria and guidelines.

Data gathering methods typically include interviews, surveys, direct observation, photography, physical measurements, and an in-depth case study approach, among others.

For the field of building (settings, spaces, facilities and urban environments) the author proposes to advance the state-of-the-art through a collection of case study examples of different building types, with a focus on universal design. These case studies (see also Preiser and Ostroff 2001) will be structured in a standardized way, including: interviews; surveys; direct observations; and videotaped walk-throughs of different facility types with various user types. The universal design critiques would focus on the three levels of performance referred to above.

UDE examples are currently under development through the Rehabilitation Engineering and Research Center at the State University of New York at Buffalo. One study focuses on wheelchair users; another, on existing buildings throughout the United States. Its Web site explains that research in more detail (www.ap.buffalo.edu).

Furthermore, methodologically appropriate ways of gathering data from populations and types of cultures with different levels of literacy and education (Preiser and Schramm, 2002) are expected to be devised. It is hypothesized that through these methodologies, culturally and contextually relevant universal design criteria will be developed over time. This argument was eloquently presented by Balaram (2001) when discussing universal design in the context of developing and industrializing nations, such as India, which he calls "the majority world".

The role of the user as "user/expert" (Ostroff, 2001) should also be analyzed carefully. The process of user involvement is often cited as central to successful universal design, but has not been systematically evaluated.

CONCLUSIONS

For mainstream architecture and the construction industry to embrace the concept of universal design, and for it to become viable and truly integrated into the building delivery and life cycle of buildings, it will be critical to have all future students in these fields familiarized with universal design. On one hand, there is the need to lay the foundation for a culture of evaluation, as eloquently argued by Preskill and Torres (1999). Obstacles to achieving this include:

• An anti-learning organization culture exists – it is reactive, not proactive.

• Leadership talks learning, but doesn't model learning.

- Communication channels and systems are under-developed or under-utilized to support organizational learning.
- Information is not willingly shared. The organization holds on to the belief that information is power, to be held by a few.
- Dialog and asking questions are not valued
- Organization members do not generally trust one another.
- There is a fear of making mistakes – risk taking is avoided.
- Independent work is more highly valued than collaborative work
- Evaluative activity is seen as threatening the status quo.
- Evaluative activity is seen as an "event."
- Evaluative activity is seen as costing too much, in terms of money, time and/or personnel resources.
- The diversity of stakeholders appears to be overwhelming.

The general fear of change permeates organizations – people are suspicious of any data collection effort.

On the other hand, there is the need to demonstrate to practicing professionals the viability of the concept through a range of UDEs, including exemplary case studies.

In the future, the "performance concept" and universal design criteria have the prospect of being made explicit and scrutinized through UDEs, and thus they will hopefully be accepted and become a part of good design practice. This will be done by moving from primarily subjective, experience-based evaluations to more objective evaluations. They will rely on explicitly stated universal design performance requirements in buildings, in the form of carefully developed programs prior to design and construction.

Critical in the notion of universal design criteria is the focus on the quality of the built environment as perceived by its occupants. In other words, building performance is seen to be a high priority beyond aspects of energy conservation, sustainability, sensitivity to the natural environment, life-cycle costing, and the functionality of buildings: universal design is simply good design which focuses on building users' perceptions and needs.

Evaluations have become more cost-effective due to the fact that shortcut methods have been devised that allow the researcher or evaluator to obtain valid and useful information in a much shorter time frame than was previously possible. Thus, the cost of undertaking universal design evaluation efforts has been considerably reduced, making UDEs more affordable.

REFERENCES

Baird, G., et al. (Eds). 1996. Building Evaluation Techniques. London: McGraw-Hill.
Balaram, S. 2001. Universal Design and the Majority World. In: Preiser, W.F.E. and Ostroff, E. (Eds). Universal Design Handbook. New York: McGraw-Hill.

Center for Universal Design.1997. The Principles of Universal Design (Version 2.0). Raleigh, N.C.: North Carolina State University.

Hock, D. 2005. One from Many: VISA and the Rise of Chaordic Organization. San Francisco: Berrett-Koehler Publishers, Inc.

Kurtz, S. 1976. "Nothing Works Best." Village Voice, August 2.

Mace, R., Hardie, G., and Place, J. 1991. Accessible Environments: Toward Universal Design. In: Preiser, W.F.E., Vischer, J.C., White, E.T. (Eds), Design Intervention: Toward a More Humane Architecture. New York: Van Nostrand Reinhold.

Maslow, H. 1948. A Theory of Motivation. Psychological Review 50, pp. 370-398.

Naisbitt, J. 2006. Mind Set! Reset your Thinking and See the Future. New York: Harper Collins.

Ostroff, E. 2001. Universal Design Practice in the United States. In: Preiser, W.F.E. and Ostroff, E. (Eds). Universal Design Handbook. New York: McGraw-Hill.

Petzinger, T. 1999. A New Model for the Nature of Business: It's Alive. The Wall Street Journal (February 26).

Preiser, W.F.E. 1983. The Habitability Framework: A Conceptual Approach toward Linking Human Behavior and Physical Environment. Design Studies 4 (No. 2).

Preiser, W.F.E, Rabinowitz, H.Z., White, E.T. 1988. Post-Occupancy Evaluation. New York: Van Nostrand Reinhold.

Preiser, W.F.E. 1991. Design Intervention and the Challenge of Change. In: Preiser, W.F.E., Vischer, J.C., White, E.T. (Eds). Design Intervention: Toward a More Humane Architecture. New York: Van Nostrand Reinhold.

Preiser, W.F.E. 1996. POE Training Workshop and Prototype Testing at the Kaiser-Permanente Medical Office Building in Mission Viejo, California, USA. In: Baird, G., et al. (Eds), Building Evaluation Techniques. London: McGraw-Hill.

Preiser, W.F.E., Schramm, U. 1997. Building Performance Evaluation. In: Watson, D., Crosbie, M.J., Callendar, J.H. (Eds). Time-Saver Standards: Architectural Design Data. New York: McGraw-Hill.

Preiser, W.F.E., Ostroff, E. (Eds). 2001. Universal Design Handbook. New York: McGraw-Hill.

Preiser, W.F.E. 2001. Feedback, Feed Forward and Control: POE to the Rescue. Building Research and Information, Vol. 29, (6) pp.456-459.

Preiser, W.F.E., Schramm, U. 2002. Intelligent Office Building Performance Evaluation. Facilities, Vol. 20, No. 7/8, pp.279-287.

Preskill, H., Torres, R.T. 1999. Building Capacity for Organizational Learning through Evaluative Inquiry. Evaluation, Vol. 5 (1), pp. 42-60.

Story, M.F. 2001. "The Principles of Universal Design." In: Preiser, W.F.E. and Ostroff, E. (Eds). Universal Design Handbook. New York: McGraw-Hill.

Vitruvius. 1960. The Ten Books on Architecture (translated by M.H. Morgan). New York: Dover Publications.

von Foerster, H. 1985. Epistemology and Cybernetics: Review and Preview. Milan: Casa della Cultura.

Watson, D., Crosbie, M.J., Callendar, J.H. (Eds) 1997. Time-Saver Standards: Architectural Design Data. New York: McGraw-Hill (7th Edition).

Young, L., Pace, R. 2001. "The Next Generation Universal Home." In: Preiser, W.F.E., Ostroff, E. (Eds). Universal Design Handbook. New York: McGraw-Hill.

LIST OF FIGURES

Credit: Author/NCARB

Figure 3: Evolving Performance Criteria
Credit: Author/Jay Yocis, University of Cincinnati

Figure 4: Universal Design versus Performance Criteria
Credit: Author/Jay Yocis, University of Cincinnati

Figure 5: Post-Occupancy Evaluation Process Model
Credit: Author/Jay Yocis, University of Cincinnati

Figure 6: Building Performance Evaluation Process Model
Credit: Author/Jay Yocis, University of Cincinnati

Figure 7: Universal Design Evaluation Process Model
Credit: Author/Jay Yocis, University of Cincinnati

JON CHRISTOPHERSEN is an architectural researcher who has been involved with dwelling standards, accessibility and universal design for the past 25 years. His work includes housing quality studies, accessibility and usability evaluation, design research on nursing homes and housing for elderly people, and recommendations for accessibility to European railways. Christophersen is also a contributor to the Universal Design Handbook and has edited an internationally acclaimed book on universal design teaching. He has presented a number of papers at international conferences, has lectured in Tokyo and at Yonsei University in Seoul and was awarded a prize for excellent paper at the Universal Design conference in Kyoto 2006.

DEVELOPMENT, PROMOTION AND EXECUTION OF UNIVERSALLY DE- SIGNED HOUSING IN NORWAY

Jon Christophersen

BACKGROUND

The story starts more than 40 years ago, with the publication of a study titled "Build for the Elderly and You Build for Life" (Boysen 1962). Not only was this an almost revolutionary concept at the time, but it also serves as a good illustration of the Norwegian approach.

The report published findings from rehabilitation projects in which researchers and disabled users combined their efforts to create highly usable solutions. As a result, the report postulated the view that accessibility ought to be integrated into the design of all new buildings. Thus, it introduced the Universal Design concept for the first time, and, importantly, as a result of user involvement in design.

The time was of course far from ready for such a revolutionary idea. The ideals of integration and inclusion were still a long way off. Instead, specially adapted housing schemes (as well as schools) were seen as the solution. Although these in no way created an atmosphere of inclusion, they did a lot to prove that people with disabilities have a chance of living independently when physical barriers are kept to a minimum. Special housing was thus an important step – in fact so important that it took almost two decades, during which the research into requirements for accessibility continued, before the next milestone was reached:

THE LIFE SPAN DWELLING

In 1982 The Norwegian Association of Disabled launched "The Life Span Dwelling" (The Norwegian Association of Disabled 1982). The Norwegian State Housing Bank had almost simultaneously (in fact a couple of months earlier), decided that Life Span housing would be rewarded by financial incentives in the form of better conditions for state subsidised loans, and laid down regulations for the design of life span standard housing. Although basically a simplified and scaled down version of requirements for wheelchair accessibility, the life span standard became the central set of guidelines for accessibility in the built environment, including performance specifications appended to the building regulations. The requirements[1] were based on guidelines for accessibility in housing published by the Norwegian Building Research Institute. Interestingly, the minimum requirements for housing became – and to a large extent still are – identical to requirements in all other building types. The rather obvious fact that requirements for housing will not be adequate in buildings used by large numbers of people has still to be fully recognised.

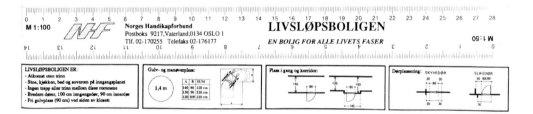

Fig. 1. *Basic requirements for life span standard include: Step free access; living room, bathroom and main bedroom on the entry floor; min 1m wide external doors and 0,9m wide internal doors; free floor space for wheelchairs at the sides of doors; turning space in the main rooms and at right angle turns; maximum gradients 1:12; 25 mm maximum height of thresholds and change of level.*

The important – and general – interpretation of these events may be rather obvious: the users possess a wealth of subjec-

---

[1] Requirements for accessibility to public buildings and blocks of flats were introduced in 1976, as an amendment to the building regulations of 1969. The regulations of 1979 had an additional requirement for accessible toilets in public buildings and a requirement for adaptability of toilets in dwellings. The latter has proved ineffectual but is still in force.

tive experience of coping with barriers in the environment. They cannot, however, (except to some extent through their organisations) be expected to voice their experience in terms of generalised requirements and objective guidelines – which of course is what the central authorities must have in order to affect policies and enact legislation. Thus, there is a need for an agent capable of constructing objective and functional performance criteria that will be understood both by politicians and the building industry.

PROMOTION OF LIFE SPAN DWELLINGS
- BOTTOM -UP AND TOP -DOWN APPROACH

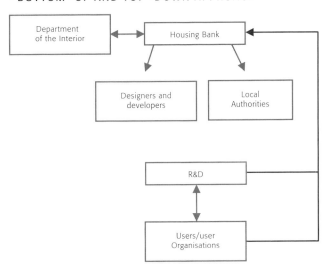

Fig. 2. Development and promotion of life span dwellings.

This was almost exactly the case as regards the life span dwelling concept. It had been constructed after years of research conducted in collaboration with (or sometimes by) the user organisations. Its factual platform was consequently solid enough to provide the groundwork that the State Housing Bank needed to promote better accessibility in housing and to persuade the government that financial incentives ought to be made available. Indeed, there can be little doubt that a large part of the success of the life span dwelling concept must be ascribed to the State Housing Bank's adoption and promotion of the idea. Not only did the Bank succeed in winning over the public, it also had success with the politicians and the building industry – a prime example of the bottom-up/top-down approach in practice.

A few notes on the Housing Bank might be necessary to understand how a state financing body can influence both the industry and the general public. As a political construct, the Bank is peculiar to Norway. Originally designed as an instrument to tackle dwelling shortages (by means of state subsidised loans), it quickly became the government's chief tool for carrying out dwelling policy. It has thus since 1949 been the country's most important force for promoting and upholding functional qualities in housing. It has financed almost 80% of the homes built since World War two and was in the early 1980s financing about 50% of all new construction.

The Bank's incentives for Life Span Housing worked: during the 1980s the proportion of life span dwellings in ordinary construction rose to and remained stable at about one half of the dwellings financed through the Bank. An unknown but possibly significant proportion of privately financed housing was also built to the same specifications – and research[2] done in the late 1990s proved that the concept was both widely known and largely well understood among the general public.

Their relative popularity notwithstanding, life span solutions only went part of the way towards more usable dwellings. By the late 1990s calculations based on statistical data showed that only about 6% of the housing stock was accessible for wheelchair users and that the percentage of usable housing could be as low as 3% (Christophersen 1996). Figures for accessibility for people with orientation problems (hearing, visual and cognitive disabilities) are not available. A wider

---

[2] Gulbrandsen and Christophersen 2002

implementation of Universal Design principles was seen as the way forward, both by central government bodies and by the user organisations.

TOWARDS UNIVERSAL DESIGN

The first efforts in the late 1990s centred on information and education. Several booklets were produced and, of more lasting importance, an education project[3] (started in 1997) inspired by the American UDEP (see Welch 1995). The education project is another example of the simultaneous top-down/bottom up approach: although organised and financed by the State Housing Bank and sanctioned by the government department for education, the user organisations and the Norwegian Building Research Institute were involved throughout.

The project involved all the schools, universities and colleges that educate professionals whose work shapes the built environment, i.e. planners, architects, designers, engineers, occupational therapists, and the building trades: joiners, plumbers, electricians etc. The project was unique in its comprehensiveness, being a co-ordinated, holistic effort towards the education of everyone and every side of the planning fields and the construction industries. The results included a series of interdisciplinary efforts and a directive that Universal Design should be included in the course plans of the relevant schools and university departments.

The logical next steps in the information/education approach were directed towards the local authorities and the building industry. The latter has been difficult to reach and the efforts in this area are still going on. Municipal authorities, however, were offered a Universal Design education package developed by the Ministry of the Environment, and a majority of the more than 400 local authorities in the country have gone through the course.

---

[3] Described in Christophersen 2002.

THE GOVERNMENT ACTION PLAN FOR INCREASED ACCESSIBILITY FOR PERSONS WITH DISABILITIES

Briefly summarised, the action plan focuses on issues concerning user participation and sector responsibility; once more the simultaneous top-down/bottom up approach is employed. The issue of sector responsibility is rather an important one, as it not only divides the tasks between the different sectors of the administration but also requires cooperation between the sectors and user involvement both as regards the different sectors and at the various stages of the planning processes. Coupled to this the action plan calls for a continuous process of evaluation, dissemination of knowledge and general information.

THE CURRENT SITUATION

Following the Department of the Environment action plan, several regions and some municipalities have drawn up and are trying to implement similar plans for their areas. Universal Design is also being brought into the legislative framework, and the Housing Bank is funding Universal Design research and Universally Designed housing projects. What is lacking – both in Norway and elsewhere – is an approach towards creating efficient, rational and practicable performance criteria for Universal Design.

LEGISLATION AND INCENTIVES FOR UNIVERSAL DESIGN

Ministries and the Housing Bank are following up the lead from the Ministry of Environment action plan. There are, however, severe problems:

- Universal Design will be introduced into the Building code, but no legal definition of Universal Design has been worked out (although the term is already used in another law).

- Requirements for Universal Design will be included in the technical section of the building regulations. This would involve strengthening the accessibility requirements, in some cases to a considerable degree. As the Norwegian accessibility requirements are among the weakest in Western Europe (Sheridan 2001), particularly as regards housing, they are nowhere near the level of usability which the definition of Universal Design presup-poses. The final outcome of the revision is unknown at the time of writing this article.

- Universal Design standards will be required for all projects financed by the Housing Bank, but the lack of precise performance criteria makes it difficult to put the requirement into practice.

The main problem, whether the legal minimum should be universally designed solutions – in housing as well as buildings for other purposes – or a lower level of accessibility, is a point that needs to be discussed. The danger is that Universal Design becomes equated with accessibility, with possibly detrimental effects to both concepts, both with regard to technical content and the wider policy issues involved. Construction cost relative to social savings due to independent living is one of the focal points of the discussion.

CURRENT SITUATION
- ACCESSIBILITY LEVELS, LEGISLATION AND UD

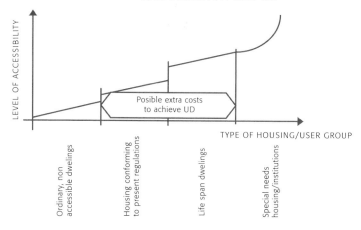

Fig. 3. Moderately increased levels of usability and accessibility can be achieved at a small and often negligible extra cost. High levels of accessibility may cost considerable amounts, due to space consumption, technical aids and construction details.

RESEARCH AND DEVELOPMENT

Presently, the State Housing Bank and the Ministry for Local Government and Regional Development initiate and fund research into:

1. *Universal Design in relation to*

- policies, political aims and goals,
- current knowledge base and competence in the construction industry,
- the relationship to other terms and conditions, such as accessibility, usability etc,
- user groups included in the definition and guidelines for Universal Design; possible limitations, contradictions and conflicts,
- functional requirements and guidelines employed in local authority approvals and involvement in planning and construction

2. Cost implications

- cost benefit/cost-cost study of the impact of Universal Design in a social context, including health and welfare aspects
- development of a method for assessing the wider cost implications of Universal Design in a social perspective
- study of Universal Design construction cost

THE PROJECT BY PROJECT APPROACH – LEARNING BY DOING

Norwegian housing comes in three broad categories:

- Detached, semi detached or terraced housing. This form of construction has for decades dominated house building everywhere outside the three main cities (Oslo, Bergen, and Trondheim).
- Small, two to four storey blocks of flats (no lifts required). These are mainly found in suburban areas around the cities, usually in the form of free standing slabs.
- Current fashion. During the past decade, making use of vacant plots for clusters of tall buildings (in the Scandinavian sense rarely more than eight storeys) on the flat roof of an underground car park has become a regular feature in the cities.

Single or two storey timber frame structures

Two to four storey blocks or flats

Concentrated developments; five or more storeys

Fig. 4. The three main categories of Norwegian housing

The Housing Bank now collaborates with architects and construction firms to achieve Universal Design in actual building projects. The approach seems to be fruitful. It not only achieves a standard close to Universal Design, but also educates and motivates the firms. An effect is that architectural details and methods of construction are developed, and tradesmen receive necessary retraining through practical work on site.

BUILT RESULTS – TWO EXAMPLES

As Universal Design is a comparatively new concept, few projects embodying it in any systematic manner have been completed; Universal Design features are most often applied haphazardly, according to the designer's whims, competence and interpretation of the legal requirements. Some projects are, however, under way:

A DETACHED HOUSE

Although this is a rehabilitation project which included conversions and an extension to a house from 1920, the example illustrates some the main features concerning the application of Universal Design principles in Norwegian housing.

ACCESS AND ENTRY

As the price of land is high and there is little vacant space on which to build, individual plots of land are by necessity small in built up regions. Thus, there is rarely more than an absolute minimum of space to park a car close to the front door.

Having the entry floor at the same level as the ground outside causes constructional problems with timber construction in locations where heavy snowfalls are normal. Many traditional homes in snow rich regions had the entry floor a metre or more above the ground outside. The present standard is about half a metre, requiring three steps, i.e. nowhere near a level access. For Universal Design the preferred solution is a flexible one, whereby level entry can be obtained by a minimum of earth works (indicated by shaded areas/white lines on fig 5) when needed.

Fig. 5. Access and entry. Main features and problems: Cramped, narrow site. Car parking close to the entry and at a level that can easily be adapted to a step free solution. A porch with minimum dimensions 1,5 x 1,5m. Slip resistant porch floor at the same level as the entry floor. Grab bars and handrails where needed

HALL AND BATHROOM

A good example of a universally designed hall is as yet close to impossible to find. Thus, a plan will have to do. The example shows a fairly spacious solution with ample space both for hanging clothes and manoeuvring wheelchairs or other aids.

The bathroom illustrates both the usual solutions and a number of typical problems:

- There is good contrast between the floor and walls, but
- the WC, the wash hand basin, taps, shower arrangement and the grab bar are all white, thus providing insufficient contrast; only white non-allergenic surface for taps and shower fittings could be obtained on the market at the time of construction. Nickel or chromium plated is standard.

Furthermore, the bathroom floor cover is not recommended

for housing; it is an industrial type developed for food preparation halls and large kitchens. Current non-slip flooring materials for dwellings are of a "sandpaper" type, which is hard to clean.

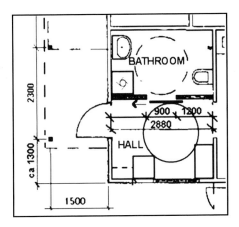

Fig. 6. Hall and bathroom. Main features: Space to manoeuvre wheelchairs. Slip resistant bathroom floor. Contrast between floor and wall surfaces. Bathroom fixtures with contrast colours and non-allergenic surfaces (as will be noticed, this requirement has not been met, as no models were on the market at the time the project was carried out).

KITCHEN

Flexible solutions are preferred. Instead of the usual fixed kitchen fittings, mobile floor units are used, and the worktop is mounted on brackets for easy height adjustment. The example also features a raised dish washing machine and (indicated by the white lines) an additional sink mounted on brackets for individual and easy height adjustment.

Fig. 7. Kitchen. Main feature: Flexibility, i.e. adjustable height work surfaces and mobile floor units.

BLOCKS OF FLATS

The example is a cluster of six blocks of flats situated on a partly underground parking area that has been slotted into a tight, rather steeply sloping site (fig. 8).

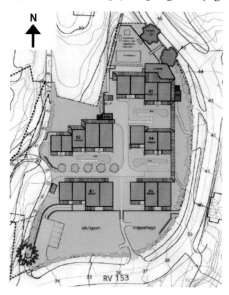

Fig. 8. Site plan

COMMUNAL OUTDOOR SPACE

Particular attention has been paid to architectural detailing, slopes and levels: Most paths are flat or gently sloping; with one exception none are steeper than 1:20, and attempts have been made to pave the walkways with functional patterning to aid orientation. The paths also have clear edge markings and there is level access from paths to play areas and recreational spaces (figs 9 and 10).

Figs. 9 and 10. External paths have patterns and edge markings to aid orientation.

PRIVATE OUTDOOR SPACE

As shown in figure 11, private open space is level with the floor inside. The same goes for the balcony floors.

Fig. 11. Level access from the flats to private open space

ENTRY

Entrance doors have contrast colours; light blue for the doors to the dwelling units, orange for the doors to the stair and lift towers (fig. 12). Whether this affords sufficient tone contrast may be debatable. Letter boxes, door bells and calling system (next to the orange door in the right hand picture in fig. 12) are positioned at accessible heights. The dwellings on the ground floor have doors directly to the outside. There is no change of level between the floor inside and the access deck or the outside pathways. Lifts connect the basement parking area to the upper floor access decks. Both the lift doors and the lift buttons have contrast colours, and the buttons are positioned within reach of a seated user. Access decks and the ground floor paved access are level with the floor inside the dwellings.

The stairs may well be the least successful element in this project, as contrast colours seem to have been forgotten (fig. 13). Stair nosings are unmarked, and better contrast may well be needed for the handrails.

Fig. 12 Blue door (left): entry to private dwelling, orange door (right) entry to stair and lift tower.

Fig 13. Contrast seems to have been forgotten when the stairs were designed. Neither the nosings nor the handrails conform to the Universal Design recommendations. For a main stair such as this, a double handrail should ideally also have been in place.

THE DWELLINGS

The plan types conform by and large to common, modern Norwegian solutions for blocks of flats: narrow rectangles with window walls on the short sides of the rectangle are divided into two zones by a middle wall parallel to the party walls. In principle, kitchen and living room functions occupy one zone. Bedroom, bathroom and hall take up the other (fig. 14).

All rooms have sufficient dimensions to allow wheelchair use, and there are no changes of level inside the dwellings. Underfloor bathroom heating has been accommodated by lowering the concrete floor slab. The kitchens are inflexible, but some – as a minimum – have a workplace that can be used by a person in a seated position. Window handles and light switches are at accessible heights, but most other electrical points are positioned near the floor (not in line with Universal Design recommendations).

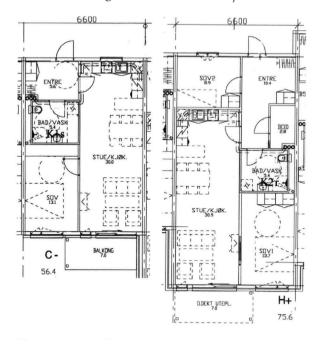

Fig. 14. Two typical floor plans; a one bedroom flat (left) and a two bedroom flat (right).

BATHROOMS

Once again, the problem of creating sufficient contrasts is evident: there is proper contrast between the floor and the walls, but all fittings are white. No provision is made for contact allergies; taps and shower are chromium/nickel plated (fig. 15).

Fig. 15. Kitchen and bathroom. Coloured bathroom fittings and non-allergenic taps and shower would have been desirable. More contrast is achieved in the kitchens, where there also is an open space underneath one of the work tops to facilitate seated users.

DOES IT WORK?

Possibly. No systematic evaluation studies of universally designed housing have as yet been undertaken. Some individual case studies – done in other contexts, but recently looked at in the context of UD/ordinary housing design (Christophersen 2006) – give good indications that both wheelchair users and people with cognitive impairments and even users with both types of disabilities can live comfortably and receive the assistance they need in universally designed housing. However, their assistance needs require a fair amount of free floor space and individual rooms for different functions (therapy, work/study etc). Thus, a small two room flat will not be sufficient for a multi handicapped or severely disabled person. There are also indications that people with very extensive disabilities, particularly those that have space consuming mobility aids and particular needs for assistance will need specially planned housing.

CONCLUSIONS

It has been a long winded, step by step process, where user requirements and research have gone hand in hand with the development of legislation, guidelines and economic incentives, which in turn have ever so slowly led to government initiatives. Importantly, there has all the time been a simultaneous bottom-up/top-down approach, not least due to indefatigable efforts by the user organisations.

In terms of concrete, built results, we have not got very far, except for a few notable examples. However, the groundwork has been done and standards, guidelines and legislation are or soon will be completed. It remains to be seen whether the concept can survive legalistic and bureaucratic meddling; there are very real dangers in this respect. So far, positive effects are that both the national association of architects and the most important developers are taking the Universal Design concept to heart and that the development and testing of efficient architectural details and planning models are taking place in parallel with on site education of the tradesmen.

REFERENCES

Boysen, C. (1962) Bygg for eldre og du bygger for hele livet (Build for the Elderly and You Build for Life). Norwegian Building Research Institute

Christophersen, J. (ed.) (2002) Universal Design – 17 Ways of Thinking and Teaching. The Norwegian State Housing Bank

Christophersen, Jon (1996): Boliger mot år 2010. Det generelle boligtilbudet. (Dwellings towards the year 2010. The conditions in the existing housing stock.) Norwegian Building Research Institute.

Christophersen, J. (2006) New Homes in The Ordinary Housing Stock - Can Universal Design Meet the Needs of Severely Disabled People? Paper at The 2nd International Conference for Universal Design in Kyoto. See Proceedings. Website: http://www.ud2006.net/en/

The Government Action Plan for increased accessibility for persons with disabilities - plan for Universal Design in key areas of society. (July 2005) See: http://www.universell-utforming.miljo.no/file_upload/hptuu_kortversjon_en.pdf

Gulbrandsen, O., Christophersen, J. (2002) Tilgjengelighet i nye boliger (Accessibility in New Dwellings) Norwegian Building Research Institute Project Report no 322.

Sheridan, L. (2001) The Control and Promotion of Housing Quality in Europe Pt. II, Comparative analysis. Housing and Policy Studies No 16, Delft University Press

The Norwegian Association of Disabled. (1982) Livsløpsboligen (The Life Span Dwelling). NHF

Welch, P. (Ed) (1995) Strategies for Teaching Universal Design. Adaptive Environments, Boston and MIG Communications, Berkeley

CREDITS

Fig 1. The Norwegian Association of Disabled (Norges handikapforbund)

Figs . 8, 14, 15 Follo boligbyggelag

All other photos and drawings by the author

A previous version of the article has been published in the proceedings of the "International Future Design Conference on Changing Places of Digi-log Future". Severance Hospital, Yonsei University, Seoul 2006.

SIGMUND ASMERVIK is a Professor at the Department of Landscape Architecture and Spatial Planning, Norwegian University of Life Sciences. He has lectured at many universities and organizations, in addition to conferences. As a researcher he has worked on topics ranging from universal design and ethic to risk assessment and management.

Sigmund has published books and articles as well as being adviser to the Norwegian government.

TEACHING UNIVERSAL DESIGN TO STUDENTS OF ARCHITECTURE

Sigmund Asmervik

INTRODUCTION
THE CONCEPT IS THE KEY

The way to the hearts and brains of students of architecture goes mainly through presentations of concrete projects in journals and presentations at their schools, and not through voluminous texts about standards and critical dimensions.

So the primary idea behind this way of introducing and teaching Universal Design is the concept of studying well known and prestigious buildings and projects.

The scope of the project is a comprehensive study analysing both outdoor areas and buildings and will thus include the work of landscape architects, architects and interior architects. The project will examine questions relating to various kinds of impairment, such as reduced mobility, hearing and vision.

It seems that prestigious architecture and architects do not pay enough attention to the needs of users. If you read the programmes and statements of juries from architecture competitions, you will be hard pressed to find text that addresses the needs of users. This is the basis for my hypothesis. You will often find words like sustainability, functionality, flexibility and, of course, aesthetics in their assessments, but these terms are mainly related to the ideas of the architect, the technological solutions and the economy of the structure, not to the special needs of persons with varying capabilities.

When I talk here of the concept of prestigious architecture, I mean buildings which have received prizes or awards for their architectural quality and buildings created by famous architects who are frequently and widely published.

HOW TO TEACH?

The main aim of this teaching approach is to give meaning to the concept of Universal Design for students in the fields of planning, architecture and landscape architecture so that as professionals they will find it an exciting and challenging part of their work.

Two aspects of the concept of Universal Design deserve special attention. One is the principle that we should plan and design for everyone without making special solutions for particular groups of the population for considerations of age or functionality. Universal Design should help to remove or at least move away from the «we and you, us and them» approach.

The second aspect is that by working with Universal Design, the students are forced to devote attention to the needs and requirements of various groups. Industrial designers are already quite familiar with this way of thinking, as they are dependent on a market that is willing to buy a product at a certain price. Architects and landscape architects have a strong tradition based on the idea that individuals' "signature projects" are the real objective of their activity, and this attitude often relegates awareness of the needs of various users to the sidelines in the learning processes.

If we focus on these two aspects, we will need to cooperate with other professions, such as occupational therapists, social workers, educators, janitors and cleaning staff.

Buildings designed by some of the most famous architects of the 20th century, such as Frank Lloyd Wright, Mies van der

Rohe, Le Corbusier and Alvar Aalto, are presented with comments in terms of Universal Design. These examples show that for quite some time architects have looked upon the ramp as an architectural element, literally creating a sliding transition from outside to inside. They have also designed such details as door handles suitable for persons of various heights.

- Barcelona has been chosen as an example of a city where truly systematic efforts are being applied to facilitate use of the city by everyone. Barcelona has been and will continue to be a magnet for students of planning and design, and, for this and a number of other reasons, will be an appropriate goal for study trips.

- The University Centre at Dragvoll in Trondheim, Norway, was planned in the 1970s. The concept on which this facility is built in many ways lends itself well to Universal Design. At the Norwegian University of Science and Technology (NTNU) in Trondheim, planners have been very aware of the need to improve access for everyone.

- 7 cases relevant for pedagogical purposes.

EXAMPLES OF GENERAL UNIVERSAL DESIGN ASSIGNMENTS

1. *How big and how small is the human body?*
   Does everybody have the same proportions? Measure each other's full length; arms, legs, height to the hips and knees. What about the proportions of children and young persons? Compare the measurements with those of Le Corbusier as they are expressed in his Modulor.

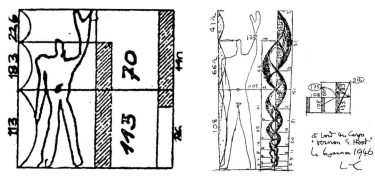

Le Modulor of Le Corbusier

2. How many people are actually functionally challenged?
Discuss in groups of four to six persons and determine
whether you have neighbours, family or friends who
are functionally challenged, who have visual or hearing
impairments or who have allergies. Try to determine the
proportion of the population that in the course of life will
have one form of functional disability or another.

3. Why is access to towns and buildings so difficult?
Try to determine why so many buildings and types of
transport are so poorly accessible. Contact the local building authorities, janitors and maintenance managers of
various organizations. Local associations for the physically
challenged may be good informants. Propose ways of en-
hancing accessibility.

UNIVERSAL DESIGN AND THE PIONEERS OF MODERN ARCHITECTURE IN THE 20TH CENTURY

During the 20s and 30s Taylorism and Fordism took the
principles of modern architecture to heart under the label of
functionalism. When the German architect Walter Gropius
established the Bauhaus, first in Weimar, 1919, and later in
Dessau, 1924, the schools of art and architecture led the way
to a new vision of modern architecture. New materials and
new constructions, together with the influence of painters

such as Mondrian, Klee and Kandinsky, were inspirations for the New Architecture.

One of the most used slogans for this new approach to architecture was *"form follows function"*. Despite what this phrase suggests, if we look back to the pioneer works by functionalists, we will find that in many ways their buildings were really not that functional at all, for instance when considering people with an impairment. But in many ways functionalism did bring elements into architecture that could be very favourable for persons with various reduced physical capacities.

The ramp as an architectural element was used frequently by many of the first generation of modernists, and the fast and effective elevator was praised by many as a good example of a modern and functional building element. I will comment here on works of some of the pioneers active in the first half of the 20th century.

This is quite the opposite of what we today include under the term Universal Design. Le Corbusier had the vision of a universal man, a white male about 183 cm in height. But today we are working to make the environment accessible to women and men of all shapes and sizes and with different capacities when it comes to moving, seeing, hearing and understanding spatial dimensions.

From these brief comments on some of the works of modernism and more specifically functionalism from some of the pioneer architects from the first half of the 20th century, we must conclude that the special needs of persons with different kinds of physical impairment were simply not on the agenda. This was the case even if the new vision of architecture claimed quite profusely that *form follows function!*

The use of the ramp, often quite steep, was more a formal gimmick than a consequence of specific design for the needs of users, while the frequent use of the modern rapid elevator was primarily the consequence of the arrival of high-rise buildings.

Reflection on design for people with visual and hearing impairments is hard to trace, and most likely this was not part of the criteria in the framework conditions for design.

LE CORBUSIER

If we start with le Corbusier, we discover that ramps have been used with great care in one of his most famous villas, Villa Savoye in Poissy, from 1928-31. Le Corbusier also made ramps a central architectonic element in a number of other buildings, often large and complex ones.

FRANK LLOYD WRIGHT

The famous Guggenheim Museum of 1959 in New York by Frank Lloyd Wright is completely designed around the spiralling inner ramp. The ramp inclination is so slight that the wall along it is used to exhibit pictures.

Frank Lloyd Wright, Guggenheim Museum, NY

MIES VAN DER ROHE

Mies van der Rohe's Barcelona pavilion from 1929 is an interesting example in this context. The generally flat floor without differences in levels expresses some of the main points of the pavilion and the new architecture, i.e. the fluent transition between inside and outside, through which persons may move easily and effortlessly. This floor level could have been made easily accessible quite simply with a slightly inclined ramp, as the differences in levels are quite modest.

Mies Van Der Rohe, Barcelona Pavilion, from 1929

ALVAR AALTO

Alvar Aalto is famous for his exquisite use of materials and the level of detailing in his buildings. Even though he did not work with the Universal Design concept, we see a number of examples in his work of his great concern for the users of buildings, whether this applies to illumination or cleaning. A special design element is his door handles at various heights for persons of various ages and heights.

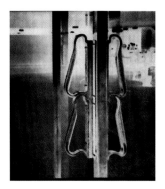

Alvar Aalto, door handles

WHAT CAN WE LEARN FROM THE HISTORY OF MODERNISM?

1. *Are famous houses from the history of architecture easily accessible?*
Find famous buildings and facilities in modern architectural history from around 1920 and later. Study their accessibility by examining blueprints and photos. The best way of becoming familiar with a building is to build a model of it.

2. *Do architectural competitions consider accessibility?*
Architectural competitions determine trends. Review a number of such competitions, and study whether the idea that buildings and facilities should be accessible to everybody has been considered.

3. *What do famous architects believe?*
Contact famous architects and landscape architects and interview them for their response to the idea that buildings should be accessible to everybody. Try to determine what they feel is the most important reason why this principle has not been carried out more than it has. Is it attitudes, finances or aesthetic considerations?

THE CITY FOR ALL
BARCELONA

Barcelona is the second largest city in Spain after Madrid. With 1.5 million inhabitants in the city and more than 5 million in the region, Barcelona is a powerful centre, from both economic and cultural perspectives, and is sometimes referred to as the heart, lungs and feet of Catalonia. Artists such as Picasso, Mirò, Tapiès, and to a lesser degree Salvador Dalí, are connected to this extraordinary city.

Dealing with architecture it is first of all Antonio Gaudì who really put his fingerprint on the city with the impressive cathedral, la Sagrada Família, the Parc Güell and those very famous dwelling houses, Casa Milà, better known as La Pedrera, and Casa Batlló on Passeig de Gràcia.

Of the younger generations Ricardo Bofill is one of the more famous and controversial architects, who among other projects also did the Barcelona airport terminal. In the last few years impressive works have been done by Jean Nouvel (Torre Agbar 2005) and Herzog, de Meuron, Gugger and Binswanger (Forum 2004).

Barcelona can also show examples of heroic city planning; the most famous is the Eixamble, the extension of the old city, by Ildefonso Cerdá. The plan goes back to the 1860s and is based on large blocks of 115 x 115 meters.

The World Exhibition in 1888 was the first in a series of large international events. At the exhibition in 1929 the famous Mies van der Rohe pavilion was the German contribution.

The Olympic Games of summer 1992 was the next big event that brought a large transformation of the city, especially along the waterfront, today named the Olympic Village. Forum 2004 was another large cultural event brought to the city.

UNIVERSAL DESIGN IN BARCELONA

For more than 15 years Barcelona has made Universal Design or Design for All, as they like to call it, a planning issue that receives special attention. In 1994 the local municipalities established a special organization to focus on the question, Consorci de Recursos I Documentaciò per a l´Autonomia Personal, usually called CRID. In this organization we might find persons with different professional backgrounds, such as architects, engineers, lawyers, designers, economists and so on.

CRID put up a strategy to make the city accessible for all, using concrete criteria, completing a plan in ten years from 1996 to 2006, and they can show impressive results from this project. They focused mostly on public open spaces: as the architect Ignasi Lecea put it, *"It is in the public open spaces that citizens learn to be citizens"*.

THE HOUSE FOR EVERYONE
THE UNIVERSITY CENTRE AT DRAGVOLL

The university centre at Dragvoll in Trondheim is part of the Norwegian University of Technology and Science, NTNU. As a special building facility it has attracted great attention and has received a number of awards for its architecture.

The architecture competition in 1971 which started the project was won by Henning Larsen's Architect Office in Co-penhagen. The winning design was based on a comparison with Oxford, England, because this has approximately the same area as the competition prospectus indicated, as much as 500,000 m2 for around 25,000 students. Today's facility is around one tenth of this.

Larsen wanted to build a dense city in a farming landscape 3–4km from downtown Trondheim. The project was based on a block structure of approximately 100 x 100 m. The most unusual aspect of the proposal was that it was based on glass-covered streets, a generally untried concept at this time in the 1970s.

Since then, glass-covered streets and urban spaces have grown quite commonplace in Norway and other parts of the world. The first section was brought into use in the autumn of 1978, the second section in the autumn of 1993, and a small third section in the autumn of 2000. Today, 2008, there are more than 2,000 students at Dragvoll and the gross area is close to 60,000 m2.

University centre at Dragvoll in Trondheim, Norway

The glass-covered streets especially have attracted a great deal of attention, and been the object of discussions, studies and research. The original main argument for this solution was its financial benefits compared to traditional streets, bearing in mind the clearing of snow and regular mainte- nance. It was later concluded that this type of design reduces energy consumption for heating and has the added advantage of creating natural meeting-places.

It later became obvious that the main concept for this facility lends itself to implementing the idea that the building and facilities should be accessible for everyone. A number of elevators are centrally placed in the streets and the facility provides a very sound basis for implementing the seven principles of Universal Design.

As regards the principles of equal opportunities for use and flexibility, we can say that this university centre is well designed. We notice this already on reaching the entrance doors, where a light push on an automatic door opener gives easy entrance. With no need for long detours to reach the destination and with clear signs, the principle of simple and intuitive use and easily comprehensible information has been well handled.

An example of the principle of tolerance of errors and design to alleviate the risk of accidents and injuries is the railing found by some stairs to prevent people with vision impairment and others from bumping their heads. The principle of generous sizes and space for access and use is enhanced by the wide streets. A curiosity is the handicap marking on a computer terminal at a height adapted to wheelchair users. This sign should really be unnecessary here!

However, even this facility features a number of details that are unsatisfactory when we consider the intention of ensuring accessibility for everyone. Measures that have been carried out to render the university centre even more accessible are listed below.

MEASURES FOR ENHANCED ACCESSIBILITY

To offer wheelchair users the opportunity to enter the building on their own and to be integrated instead of being sitting exhibits at a show, automatic entrance doors were installed in entrances adjacent to the parking area for the physically challenged. Additionally, new door opening buttons and new display panels were installed by the elevators inside the buildings to enable wheelchair users to use the facilities on their own. Not all the elevators are accessible, but wheelchair users have access to all areas, even though in some locations they must choose one out of two elevators. Study desks have been reserved close to these elevators.

All regular exit doors have been replaced by sliding doors with infrared sensors. This eases accessibility for all users. The information desk has been furnished with hatches at a height suitable for wheelchair users and with bells for summoning assistance.

All auditoriums are being adapted for wheelchair users. Some auditoriums had a high brick wall which wheelchairs users were unable to see over, and this has now been replaced by tables so that wheelchairs users are able to sit with the others. All the auditoriums feature adjustable tables intended for wheelchair users. All stairs in the walkways are marked so that they are visible for those with vision impairment. Induction loops for the hearing impaired have been installed in all the auditoriums. Maps on the outside of auditoriums indicate the parts of the rooms that have good coverage.

All staircases in communal areas are marked with white tiles on vertical and horizontal planes. Eventually all the areas will be marked in contrasting colours. Outside markings and opening buttons have been placed on an attractive standard column so that they can be used by anyone.

EXAMPLES OF ASSIGNMENTS ON "BUILDING FOR ALL"

1. *How can we study whether a building is accessible to everyone?*
   Undertake a specific and detailed study of accessibility for persons with mobility, vision and hearing impairments and/or allergies in a building used by a large number of

people. Interview the maintenance department and the staff working with health, environment and safety issues. Propose improvements and draw up a detailed plan for improvement works.

2. *How can we plan to improve accessibility?*
In an exercise assume that a building, park or facility must be accessible for everyone. Consider how you can exploit ramps and elevators, colour and lighting as architectural techniques/measures.

3. *What do architects think about buildings they themselves have planned?*
Visit and interview architects and landscape architects and find out what they think about their own work. It is useful to undertake some research at the locations in question so that you can ask the really penetrating questions.

SEVEN PROJECTS WITH INTERESTING PEDAGOGICAL POTENTIAL

Here seven projects will be presented and discussed with reference to the principles of Universal Design as relevant cases for teaching students of architecture. Most of them are from the mid 90s and onward. One exception is the Sydney Opera House by the Danish architect Jørn Utzon which started its long road to realization in the late 1950s. Observations and comments are based on my own visits to the buildings during the period from autumn 2002 to spring 2006. There might be some changes in some of the buildings since I did my study trip, but for pedagogical reasons I do not think this matters very much. The projects are:

1. Sydney Opera House by Jørn Utzon, 1957–1973

2. Museum of Contemporary Art, Barcelona, by Richar Meier, 1995

3. Guggenheim Museum, Bilbao, by Frank Gehry, 1997

4. The Parliament Building in Berlin, by Norman Foster, 1999

5. The Jewish Museum in Berlin, by Daniel Libeskind, 2001

6. The Telenor Corporation Office Building in Oslo, by HUS architects, NBBJ Architects Norway and architect Per Knudsen, 2001

7. The Niteroy Area in Rio de Janeiro, by Oscar Niemeyer, 2004.

SYDNEY OPERA HOUSE

Sydney Opera House has been in the headlines of newspapers and architectural journals for decades. As winner of a famous international architectural competition, it has received much attention over the years. The long political and not least economic dispute over this project has kept new aspects of it alive for more than four decades. But I had never seen or heard of any comments on the accessibility of the building before I made my personal investigations in the autumn of 2002.

Arriving along the waterfront from the Circular Quay area in downtown Sydney, you are quite impressed by the characteristic roof forms of the building, reminding you of sails on a ship at sea. Some hundred meters from the enormous stairs, you notice a very visible sign telling wheelchair users to take the left lane along the waterfront and in doing so you leave a smooth stone surface and bobble along a cobblestone path, not very pleasant or practical for a wheelchair user. After going 30 to 40 metres you are led to a lower level via a ramp, a little more than one metre lower and in a dark corner under a concrete deck, where you find a nicely designed brass door with a button to push, and with a very small sign saying:

Access for disabled to opera. Press button for assistance and await reply.

We could excuse this by trying to say that this represents the attitudes of half a century ago. But I am not too sure that this is really a good excuse. Another interesting feature of the Sydney Opera House is the huge area with stairs, said to be inspired by American Indian pyramids, with no contrasts marking the stairs and no sufficient handrails. This shows an almost grotesque lack of understanding of the capabilities of all users of the building.

Sydney Opera House

MUSEUM OF CONTEMPORARY ART, BARCELONA

Barcelona is quite famous for its design for all public open-space projects, public buildings and collective transport. The idea of making the city more accessible got a huge lift when it hosted the Olympic Games in 1992. This was the first time in history that the Paralympics were held in the same arenas as the Olympics.

So when Richard Meier was planning and designing a new Museum of Contemporary Art in Barcelona, which was opened in 1995, he was obviously inspired by the idea of looking at the access, entrance and use of the building for all persons, including those depending on transport with wheels, such as prams, wheelwalkers and wheelchairs. With a smooth stone surface outside and a very slight gradient up to the entrance of the building, the first impression is promising. And inside, a very visible ramp system takes you to the various levels in the building. But for persons with impaired vision, the building is completely unusable. Painting walls, ceilings and columns all white is one of the trademarks of Richard Meier's architecture. Quite obviously this makes the building very difficult to move in, even for people with normal sight; as there are only slight or no contrasts, and there are large glass areas in the main facade, you feel dazzled in many areas of the museum.

Entering the handicapped toilet or the elevator you are also challenged in the first case by a white bathroom with little contrast whereas the all black elevator makes it difficult to see anything in the very small elevator space.

Museum of Contemporary Art, Barcelona

GUGGENHEIM MUSEUM IN BILBAO

For almost ten years hordes of visitors have headed for Bilbao with the main aim of visiting the Guggenheim Museum designed by Frank Gehry. Certainly a nice large edifice by the river, but what is the functionality of the building like? The main entrance is really a challenge for everyone, especially making your way down the numerous steps which are designed so cleverly to make it look as if all the people entering the museum have just been through hip-replacement surgery, because the relation between the height and depth of the stairs is so poorly proportioned.

As we see in the figure a long area of stairs just outside the building needs special support measures because the stairs are so poorly designed.

At the top of the descending stairs to the main entrance is a nicely designed sign telling visitors that the building is also accessible to persons in wheelchairs, but please enter from the secondary entrance down by the river. This is not a half century ago, as with the Sydney Opera House, but the autumn of 2005.

I could not find any sign of design sympathetic to persons with reduced sight, the design of the door handles was far from perfect and there was no sign of contrast marking on the stairs.

Guggenheim Museum in Bilbao

Poorly designed stairs

THE PARLIAMENT BUILDING IN BERLIN

The Germans brought Norman Foster all the way from London to design the remodelling of the very symbolic Reichstag in Berlin. The main concept of his proposal was to construct a glass dome over the central part of the building. In addition to reaching the top by elevators, you can make the trip the whole way up via a spiral ramp.

This is a very good example of how the ramp as an architectural element can be used in a very exciting way, and it is also very accessible if you depend on wheeled transport. Access through the main entrance up several stairs is more difficult for anyone with a physical impairment. There is a secondary wheelchair entrance typical of the remodelling of many old historic buildings.

The spiral ramp

THE JEWISH MUSEUM IN BERLIN

Another fairly new building in Berlin which has received much attention and been discussed and reviewed in most architectural journals in the world is the Jewish Museum designed by Daniel Libeskind. The new museum is an extension of a historic building. It is worth looking at this to see how successful the new extension is in relation to the old building. The main entrance to the complex is through the old building. Many historic buildings have a main floor one or two metres above the ground, and back in history horse-drawn carts were the most common means of transport. So the ramp was already there, but the surface was often not very smooth; often cobblestones were used. The Libeskind solution is quite elegant with parts of the ramps with smooth stones and the rest with cobblestones.

So much for adaptation to persons using wheelwalkers and wheelchairs. Once inside the building you notice that not much attention has been paid to vision impairment in the solutions. Quite characteristically, as you find in many modern buildings, they have safety step markers that create a colour contrast, here with black tape on a grey floor. But especially dangerous is the fact that there is just a one-step difference between two levels in public areas where hundreds of visitors are walking about, as is typical in a museum.

The main entrance

Black tape on a grey floor

THE TELENOR CORPORATION OFFICE BUILDING

The Telenor office building just outside Oslo was given an AIA (American Institute of Architects) prize in 2003, one of just a few European buildings to receive this award. That caught my attention and I decided to take a closer look at the building to see if the principles of Universal Design had been followed.

The result was much the same as in most modern buildings. The architects have to follow the existing building codes, so elevators and wide doors which open automatically are part of the design. One interesting issue was discovered in a large auditorium that had been designed for wheelchair users as attendees of lectures and other performances. But the day a wheelchair user was going to make a presentation, an acute problem arose because there was no access to the podium for the speaker.

Yet another design trap is the one-to-three stair difference in level, running over 60 metres across a large plaza, where there already have been quite a few accidents.

Also here we noted a lack of attention to persons with visual impairments as there was no contrast marking on stairs and the interior architect had not taken colour blindness into consideration when designing the office workspaces.

The Telenor Complex

Dangerous steps

OSCAR NIEMEYER AT NITEROY

One hour's drive outside the centre of Rio de Janeiro, in Niteroy, the famous Brazilian architect Oscar Niemeyer has planned a large area for various cultural activities; a museum of contemporary art, a cinema centre, a chapel, both a Catholic and a Baptist cathedral, a theatre and a memorial building for a former governor of Rio de Janeiro. Of these buildings, only the art museum and the memorial hall have been built. Typical of many of the buildings Oscar Niemeyer has planned is that they are accessed by ramps with different designs, very often curved ramps, which give a very elegant entrance to the buildings, quite the opposite of the very poor design of the entrance to the Bilbao Guggenheim Museum.

Despite the frequent use of entrance ramps, the architect appears to have lost sight of the purpose as access inside the building for persons with reduced movement ability is not good. Typically, as soon as you pass through the entrance door you are often met by steps if you want to go further into the building. So the frequent use of ramps seems mainly to be an architectural, not a functional, feature, but on the other hand it demonstrates very clearly that the ramp can be a very important architectural element.

Outdoor ramps

SUMMARY

With the introduction of modernism during the last two decades of the 19th century and with the definition of a new architecture through functionalism, it would be reasonable to expect design supporting all men and women, whatever their level of physical ability. But no, the Modulor developed by Le Corbusier clearly demonstrates a view quite opposite to the understanding of Universal Design today. Instead of looking for universal man, and it really was "man" not "woman", we are today focusing on designing the universal environment for very different human beings. The drive and impetus leading us in this direction, the right to live an independent life, has definitely not so far come from the prestigious architects and their work.

Yet even if the heroes of functionalism failed in many ways, they still can inspire young students to have the vision of cities and buildings for all. Looking at seven projects by prestigious architects from mid 20th century, the Sydney Opera House and up to the turn of the century, we register with some surprise that there is still some road ahead to make these buildings closer to the ideal of Universal Design.

But still I think it is worth while to focus on these kinds of "masterpieces" when introducing the principle of Universal Design to students of architecture, because it is a fact that the students of architecture primarily have these kinds of projects as their ideal.

REFERENCES

Asmervik. S., 2001, Byer, hus og parker for alle. Institutt for landskapsplanlegging, UMB ,Aas.

Asplan Viak, 2003, Telenor Park and Central Court, Byggekunst, no 1, 2003, Oslo

Asmervik. S, Cold, B., Fathi, H., 1999, Evaluering vi, den overdekte gaten pd Dragvoll. SINTEF-rapport. Trondheim.

Deutsches Architektur Museum, 2003, Oscar Niemeyer, A legend of modernism, Birkhäuser

Dollens, D. & Meier, R., 1998, Barcelona Museum of Contemporary Art, Monacelli Press

Drew, P., 2000, Utzon and the Sydney Opera House, Annandale, New South Wales, Inspire Press

Foster, N. & Schulz, B., 2000, The Reichstag: Sir Norman Foster's Parliament Building, Prestel, Munich

Gehry, F., 2001,Guggenheim Museum, Harry N. Abrams Publ.

Gonzalez, A and Lacuesta, R., 2001, Barcelona Architecture Gustavo Gili SA, Barcelona.

NBBJ arch., HUS arch. & PKA arch., 2003, Telenor New Headquarter, Fornebu, Byggekunst, no 1, 2003, Oslo

Rappolt, M. & Violette, R. , 1999, Gehry Draws, The MIT Press

Schneider, B., 1999, Daniel Libeskind, Jewish Museum Berlin, Prestel, Munich

CAMILLA RYHL holds a Masters and Ph.D. degree (2003) in Architecture from the Royal Danish Academy of Fine Arts in Copenhagen. Her Ph.D. "A House for the Senses" is a study on housing design for people with sensory disabilities. She has continued specialising in accessibility as a Postdoctoral Fellow, researching and teaching Universal Design in the Architecture Department at UC Berkeley (2003-2006), where she was also a Fulbright Scholar (2000-2001). She is currently a Senior Researcher in the Accessibility Unit at the Danish Building Research Institute. She specializes in housing research, sensory impairments and Universal Design.

ARCHITECTURE FOR THE SENSES
Camilla Ryhl

INTRODUCTION

Accommodating sensory disabilities in architectural design requires specific design considerations. These are different from the ones included by the existing design concept Accessibility, which accommodates physical disabilities. Hence a new design concept *Sensory Accessibility* is presented as a parallel and complementary concept to the existing one.

Sensory accessibility accommodates sensory disability and describes architectural design requirements needed to ensure access to the sensory experiences and architectural quality of a given space. While the existing concept of accessibility ensures everyone of physical access to a given space, sensory accessibility ensures that everyone can stay in the space and be able to participate, enjoy and experience.

This article is based on research findings from a PhD dissertation titled A House for the Senses, a study of architectural requirements in housing design implied by a sensory disability. The empirical research project is based on qualitative interviews and 1:1 testing in existing housing with a group of people living with a sensory disability. The participants were either blind, deaf, partially sighted or hard-of-hearing. A control group also participated.

BACKGROUND

Sooner or later in life, we will all experience living with impaired vision or hearing. We will either ourselves experience losing the ability to see or hear or a family member or friend will experience chronic or temporary vision or hearing loss.

Our physical environment is designed with the average person in mind and without consistent consideration of human diversity. Regardless of whether impairment is congenital or acquired by trauma, it may therefore be extremely difficult to manage even basic daily activities, communicate or find our way in the physical environment.

Even with available assistive technology, managing daily tasks in a familiar environment requires great physical and mental resources for a person living with a sensory disability. This includes a familiar environment like your own home, where the resources needed to perform these tasks are mentally strenuous to a degree that has no equivalent in the lives of people with no sensory impairment (Karlsson, 1999). Most people think that people living with a visual or hearing impairment can easily "manage" in ordinary housing, but it is not a matter of it being possible or not, but rather of why anyone should settle for just "managing". Having requirements and wishes for architectural quality and aesthetic pleasure in the dwelling which constitutes one's home is a universal need unrelated to physiological ability or sensory disability.

Basic architectural elements such as daylight, acoustics and spatial proportions are of decisive importance for the communication and architectural experience of people with impaired vision or hearing (Ryhl, 2003). By working consciously with these elements, it is possible to design dwellings where the basic architectural design accommodates a sensory impairment and decreases the need for assistive technology, rather than a design that implies hard work to navigate through and live in every day.

THE SENSES AND THE EXPERIENCE OF ARCHITECTURE

We are always and constantly present in this world as we move through, over, under and towards our surroundings. We see, hear, feel, smell, sit, move and taste our way through our immediate world every day and all the time. Asleep or awake, we constantly perceive form, size and texture of that which our body experiences directly or indirectly. Our senses never rest, our vision opens up the world to the stars and the skin senses the almost invisible splinters in wooden surfaces. Consciously or subconsciously we constantly receive information about the world we are in. Our body is active in the process, as when we move up and down stairways, lean against stone walls warm from the sun, sit on a curb or walk through open doors. Or our body is the passive recipient of perceptions, as when the breeze from a window blows through the space and softly touches our skin, or we hear the banging of the open door upstairs. Whether we are active or inactive in the process, our senses never cease to perceive and they are inextricably linked with our perception of space, form and architecture. So what happens if one of our senses is impaired or disabled?

In modern time Aristotle's classic definition of our five senses is being challenged by various new classifications, such as Gibson's fivesense-system (Bloomer and Moore, 1977) and Pallasmaa's model of the seven senses (Pallasmaa, 1996). In the context of architecture, vision and touch traditionally dominate, although a few architects emphasise the importance of the sense of hearing (Eiler Rasmussen, 1957, Pallasmaa 1996) and the kinaesthetic sense (Moore and Bloomer 1977, Pallasmaa 1996) in the experience of architecture. Existing research on how people living with a sensory disability experience architecture shows that five sense categories are important: vision, hearing, touch, smell and the kinaesthetic sense/ balance (Ryhl, 2003).

Depending on the nature and degree of the sensory disability in question, different senses compensate for the impaired one. Design requirements and the perception of architectural quality reflect the increased use of the remaining senses and the need for considering sensory accessibility as an architectural element.

Universal Design versus Performance Criteria

VISION

With our sense of vision we register light, shape, surface, colour, structure, perspective and depth. Vision registers the entirety as well as the fragment. Without vision we can sense objects within a maximum radius of 30 m, but with vision we can see all the way to the stars. Vision also breaks down the boundaries of time and space due to its unlimited sense radius. Vision notifies us about what is ahead and in that way vision spans across time and into the future.

In modern western culture vision is considered our primary sense and as seeing persons 85-90% of the stimuli we rely on are based on visual perception. Vision is in particular connected to the sense of touch and to hearing, to which, however, vision is superior, since humans will typically try to confirm visually the information they receive via the senses of touch and hearing. Vision is also strongly connected with the senses of balance and kinaesthesia. A child exploring the world watches objects from several angles and thereby forms the basis of experience that will later enable it to identify the objects, independently of angle or dimensions.

People living with impaired hearing depend on vision as their primary sense. Increased awareness of visual stimulation results in increased sensitivity to visual noise, the visual equivalent of acoustic noise. Too much flickering, waving or motion in the visual field causes a disturbance or interruption; the result is the same as noise for a hearing person. You lose focus and often become frustrated and fatigued if the visual noise is not removed.

Vision dissolves spatial definitions, e.g. between indoors and outdoors, via transparent surfaces and open transitions. But vision also emphasises connections and dissipates feelings of isolation and loneliness. Pallasmaa says: "The eye is the sense of distance and separation", and studies have shown that the visual connection to what is outside the space we are in is crucially important to the sense of being part of a greater context (Ryhl, 2003). A space that does not provide visual contact with the horizon or surrounding context increases the feeling of isolation and loneliness. This phenomenon is most significant for deaf people, who particularly need to register visually what they cannot hear. But visually impaired persons also emphasise the importance of both physical and acoustic connection to the world outside their home for social (Percival, Hanson and Osipovic, 2006) as well as existential reasons (Ryhl, 2003).

Light gives form and structure: its contrasts emphasise elements and surfaces. Light is a prerequisite for seeing but also for tactile experiences of warmth and comfort. For blind or visually impaired persons, hearing becomes the primary sense, but touch is a decisive secondary sense and daylight an essential source of pleasure as well as information about time.

The character of the light in a space, whether direct or re-flected, makes varying demands on the adaptation abilities of the eye, and seeing people will generally adjust effortlessly. However, depending on the nature of the impairment, some might be limited by an impaired ability of the eye to adapt and thus find it difficult to navigate through contrasts or sudden changes of light. Adjusting in order to orient oneself requires time and change of pace.

HEARING

Hearing transcends physical space and senses activities and information far beyond our own body space and field of vision. Hearing dissolves physical barriers and moves across space.

Hearing plays a significant role in orientation. From the centre of our body, which is experienced as a vertical central axis at the front, we are able to localise sound sources and use them in our orientation. We register acoustic sound marks and use them in our orientation. We establish an acoustic dialogue with a space, when we send out our own sounds in order to read the form and character of the space via the acoustic information that the space sends back.

Hearing is inextricably linked with the kinaesthetic sense, as there is no sound without movement. We send out sounds in order to hear; we clap our hands or sing in order to fully enjoy the grandeur and immensity of the cathedral, feeling that only when sound fills the space does it come alive. On the other hand, the soundlessness of a space emphasises our own sounds, and suddenly our own steps and breathing become pronounced and the stillness of the space accentuates our sense of existence. Stillness is not necessarily just the absence of sound, but rather also an expression of another kind of concentration, a shift of focus, a change in pace. A space can hold a quiet quality or it can be too overwhelming in its silence. Pallasmaa says: "A powerful architectural experience silences all external noise; it focuses our attention on our very existence, and as with all art, it makes us aware of our fundamental solitude."

Just like the other sense organs the ear has amazing adaptation abilities. To protect ourselves against the immense amount of sensory stimuli that we are constantly exposed to, we subconsciously adjust our hearing while accommodating to the sounds around us. When we are bombarded with sounds in all contexts we tune out our hearing in order to function, and thus in the middle of the acoustic confusion we lose sound experiences that could have been positive. Conscious acoustic planning and design of our physical settings would prevent this tendency. "Our ears have been blinded", Pallasmaa says about our contemporary anechoic buildings and monotonous sound landscapes in public spaces.

The ability to adapt is also the reason why some people seem to have better hearing than others although in reality they are merely more aware of their acoustic perceptions. This is the case with people who live with vision impairment; for blind people hearing is the primary sense.

For blind people in particular, hearing plays a primary role in orientation and the importance of hearing is far greater to this group than to seeing people; "Several descriptions indicate that hearing to the blind seems to some degree to have another "function" than that to the sighted, and the use of this sense to identify objects probably lacks its counterpart for the sighted." Hearing is the unquestioned primary sense for blind and visually impaired people, and the acoustics of any given space are therefore crucial for the quality of any architectural experience for these user groups, as well as people who are hard-of-hearing (Ryhl, 2003).

Although the majority of people remain unaware of most of their acoustic perceptions, we store them in our body and react to them physically. People who are particularly dependent on their hearing also live with an increased acoustic sensitivity and a higher risk of physical discomfort related to acoustic experiences. They often experience inability to participate in activities and conversations because the acoustics of a given space cause physical discomfort and pain.

Hearing not only affects our physical comfort but also plays a significant role in communication, which means it is a significant social factor. Our primary means of communication in verbal and for people with impaired hearing the acoustic quality of a given space is crucial to the outcome of verbal information, conversation and experiences. Even though body language forms a major part of communication many nuances and details are conveyed through our vocal pitch and intonation, and persons with impaired hearing often find themselves excluded and lonely in social contexts. Hence hearing affects both the spatial and the social experience of our existence.

TOUCH

With touch we experience form, structure, texture and temperature. With touch we are limited to registering what is within the reach of our own body. We sense fragments corresponding to the length of our reach, fragments which are put together as an entirety via the cognitive process.

Our body is one large sensory surface; with our fingertips we feel a single grain of sand, our feet register the vibrations of the floor and with our whole body we enjoy the warmth of the sun and the touch of water. The sense of touch is so fundamental to our perception of the world, and the hand especially is so active that some people consider it a sensory organ in its own right. Pallasmaa believes that all the other senses can be considered as extensions of the sense of touch. "The eyes want to collaborate with the other senses. All the senses, including vision, can be regarded as extensions of the sense of touch; the senses are specialisation of the skin. The senses define the interface between the skin and the world, the interface between the opaque interiority of the body and the exteriority of the world."

The sense of touch is the most important sense of all in our experiences of the physical environment. It is via the sense of touch that we first experience the world, discover and identify objects and contexts. The sense impressions we receive when as small children we slowly expand our world by touching everything, tasting and feeling it with our hands, body and mouth are all stored in the body. This way the child creates the cognitive basis of reference in order to recall the feeling of the object when he sees, hears or smells it later in life. We identify the objects from our recollection of the sense of touch.

The tactile identification ability of our feet is connected with our sense of orientation and is reciprocally important to the sense of balance and the kinaesthetic sense. The sense of touch is closely connected with vision, which is for example seen when we are visually attracted to the texture or structure of a surface and we instinctively reach out to touch it; the sense of touch has to confirm what we see. When parents touch their newborn baby, it stimulates the baby's bodily awareness, which in turn creates the foundation of experiences to help it perceive its own bodily interfaces and coordinates later on.

The sense of touch is significant for blind and visually impaired persons, since it (like hearing) compensates for the lack of vision. As described, we register the world in fragments which we add to form an entirety. This phenomenon is particularly noticeable in blind people who put the perceived fragments together in the chronological order of experience, because they lack the visual supplement to tactile perceptions. In a way, they sense in a sequential time line. Karlsson describes this in his phenomenological investigations of the life of a blind person, "When a blind person describes his active perception experience it shows how object identification occurs in stages through sense impressions in the form of *sense impressions, knowledge, conclusion*." Moreover, he emphasises how important it always is to orient, even in the case of a familiar space. "The sense impressions are mostly of a tactile nature but they can also be auditory or based on smell impressions. The experience of "I'm here" requires a memorized knowledge of the surroundings and a cognitive process before you can move on to the next direction finder or the end destination. Moving around thus relies on cognitively known chains of "here and now" and "if I do like this" it brings me to "that, and so on". It is so mentally exhausting for the blind to orient and move around in familiar and known surroundings, that there is no equivalent for the sighted." Research supports this finding, as visual disability requires extreme mental resources in order to navigate or just move through physical space. Regardless of it being familiar or unfamiliar space, it always requires hard work.

For deaf persons and persons with impaired hearing, the sense of touch is also decisive. Through vibrations in both wall and floor surfaces information is perceived about what is not seen. Basically what cannot be heard must be seen, but as this limits perception to the field of vision, the tactile information offered by the architectural design is decisive in knowing what happens outside the field of vision.

SMELL

The sense of smell is one of the strongest in the process of recollection; one may say the nose reminds the eye of forgotten experiences. However, contemporary society almost makes a virtue of diminishing the sense of smell in our sensations. While hearing is exposed to extreme sensory inputs and therefore needs to adjust by "turning down", we are consciously focused on eliminating natural sense stimulations in our time and culture. We surround ourselves with synthetic scents to decrease our natural odours, and thus our sense of smell is more or less anaesthetised.

People living with impaired vision or hearing have increased awareness of their smell perceptions. Smell impressions are used as means of orientation and smell marks are used in the same way as sound marks for hearing people and land marks for seeing people.

BALANCE AND THE KINAESTHETIC SENSE

The kinaesthetic sense registers the position and movement of our limbs, muscles and tendons as well as the position of the body itself. The kinaesthetic sense is essential for our experiences of space and architecture. As we move our body through, over, in, under, towards and away from the spaces that we encounter, the kinaesthetic sense, along with our balance, ensures that our body movements reflect the size and shape of the space. The kinaesthetic sense controls the way we move our eyes to see, our hands to feel and our feet to sense when we experience space. The kinaesthetic sense ensures our perception of surfaces, structures, levels and gaps. Our body stores our kinaesthetic experiences, and therefore we move easily up and down stairs without looking at the steps, because the body knows exactly how high we need to lift our feet in order to take the next step.

It only takes a few deviations from the norm to surprise the body and turn the subconscious movement into awareness of our position in space e.g. a couple of stepping-stones that are not aligned or a staircase with uneven steps. The architect can use very small means to direct the user's concentration and consciousness.

Awareness of the body's position in relation to itself and its surroundings is based on the perceptions of the senses of balance, hearing, touch, vision and kinaesthesia. But the significance of the kinaesthetic sense to the experience of our own body is so great that even if we were blinded and deafened and were not allowed to use our sense of touch, we would still be able to establish an experience of our bodily position in space and of the interrelation of the individual parts of our body.

The sense of balance registers movements and orientation of the head in relation to gravity and other directions, and like the kinaesthetic sense it is stimulated by sensory inputs from the body itself. Balance is essential to the constitution of our bodily position in relation to the space and the body itself, and it ensures a constant and unchangeable sense of vertical and horizontal directions and movements. When the sense of balance is challenged, we lose our sense of direction and need a point of reference to re-establish the order of the space and the body within it.

As the centre of balance lies within the inner ear, many people with impaired hearing also have problems with balance, and Ménière's disease in particular is an example of such damage. Balance is also connected to vision; a visual experience that challenges our perspective or manipulates our sense of depth is a problem for some. A wavy floor surface or flickering patterns may trigger a balance upset causing extreme cases of vertigo for some. Visual noise may cause the same effect for some. The sense of balance is yet another sense that the architect can challenge and provoke consciously to achieve the desired experiences, although the consequences are not always desired by everyone.

"Every touching experience of architecture is multi-sensory; qualities of matter, space and scale are measured equally by the eye, ear, nose, skin, tongue, skeleton and muscle. Architecture strengthens the existential experience, one's sense of being in the world, essentially giving rise to a strengthened experience of self."

As we see, hear, smell, feel and move in the world every day, it is our body and senses that lead us through the encounter. All our senses constantly perceive our surroundings and it is debatable whether it is even possible to distinguish between the senses in the process or whether they are actually so closely connected and mutually complementary that our encounter with the world arises in the synergy of them all. They incessantly receive information by way of stimuli. Via a complex process in the central nervous system and the brain, the information is examined cognitively and we are able to recognise and identify spaces and objects around us. Some sense impressions remain subconscious, but they are still stored in the body and memory, and we are able to recall them when needed.

We live out of our experience, and we repeat our own patterns, because it is what we know. We identify space and context from our existing knowledge, and our perception of the world is based on the experiences we carry within us. Thus our experience and characterisation of space and architecture are based on our inherent physical, mental and sensory knowledge and at the same time on our physiological abilities. The environmental psychologist E.T. Hall says "Man learns from what he sees, and what he learns influences what he sees."

We cannot separate the experience of space and sensory ability, or separate the characterisation of space from our inherent physiological experience. Hence, a sensory impairment implies specific requirements for a sensory-accessible architecture.

SENSORY DISABILITY AND ACCESS TO THE EXPERIENCES OF ARCHITECTURE

In order to create not only physical accessibility of the built environment, but also to ensure accessible sensory experiences of architectural quality for everyone, the architect needs to incorporate specific design considerations. As visual and hearing impairments imply the use of different remaining senses, the required design considerations vary accordingly.

VISUAL IMPAIRMENT

For blind or visually impaired people, spatial proportions are essential as the volume and in particular the size of a space must not be overwhelming to the user. This is explained by two things; it is important to be able to reach a point of reference within just a few steps and large volume spaces generally have a very high reverberation time leading to perceived negative acoustic quality. For a blind person or someone with low vision, it is difficult to navigate as well as "read" the general layout of a space without using the sense of touch. The acoustics are used to "read" and understand its size, but both perceptions are needed for understanding the general layout and size. It is easy to feel lost and helpless without a point of reference and research shows that as soon as reverberation time exceeds 0.6 - 0.7 sec the acoustics are perceived as uncomfortable, stressful and not helpful for understanding the architectural design. A comfortable reverberation time is also needed to accommodate communication and social activities. One must be able to hear what cannot be seen.

Acoustics and spatial proportions are mutually interrelated. The solution to creating a large and acoustically comfortable space is not necessarily to adjust acoustically, as it is important to this user group that the acoustics convey the needed information of size and proportions. A large space needs to sound large. Hence proportions and acoustics must be mutually reflective.

It is nonetheless also important that the reverberation time does not exceed 0.6 - 0.7 sec in order to minimise physical and psychological discomfort, assure a general comfort zone for communication and a sensory-accessible architectural space.

For reasons of psychological and physical comfort daylight

is essential. Regardless of visual impairment and degree of remaining sense of vision or sense of light, daylight is a high priority for everyone. It is a source of warmth, as a guiding landmark and as a supporting feature of communication. In the dwelling a visually impaired person may very consciously move around in the house in order to follow the daylight and place herself where direct daylight falls in the room. Daylight is regarded as a quality and as such a source of comfort and well being. Visually impaired people have varied lighting requirements depending on the nature and degree of their disability and they require a different context to unfold. But a conscious and considered use of daylight is required to prevent physical discomfort for everyone. Windows and other openings are also essential connections to surrounding spaces, whether indoors or outdoors. Being constantly as-sured of existing in a larger context than the immediate per-ceptible one is crucial to everyone and for visually impaired this information must be communicated through hearing and touch. Windows and openings are also important guid-ing marks in orientation, as they function both as zones of increased light, which is helpful to people with a remaining sense of vision, and as acoustical points of navigation.

IMPAIRED HEARING

A general feeling of being restricted spatially is prevalent when you are deaf or hearing impaired. This brings a deci-sive need for large spacious rooms, almost as if the spatial volume cannot be large enough. This user group introduces the concept of "body space" as an architectural feature, de-scribing the need for large volume spaces, a constant visual connection to the world outside, in particular to the sky and horizon, and a general sense of openness.

As people with impaired hearing also have increased acoustic sensitivity the need for large volume spaces implies a basic dilemma, as this user group, like the visually impaired, perceives large spaces as having negative acoustic qualities. Basically this requires the architect to work with an increased focus on the acoustical aspects of his architectural designs. Acoustic sensitivity in this user group seems to imply an acceptable reverberation time as low as 0.4 sec, which might in turn be challenging to people with normal hearing. Research showed the decisive role of the reverberation time for this user group as it completely outweighed other qualities otherwise described as important. An example would be a space being perceived as spacious, open and of great visual quality but assessed as a "useless and uninhabitable" space because the reverberation time was too high.

Deaf people may have lost their sense of hearing, but their sense of sound is not necessarily impaired. This means acoustic information is not necessarily inaccessible to deaf people at all. Acoustic information on activities outside the field of vision can be communicated through vibrations in wall and floor surfaces. If the architectural design accommodates this tactile perception of acoustic stimulations, deaf users are ensured sensory accessibility to acoustic experiences.

Daylight and visual connections are also essential. Particularly for deaf users, windows are crucial and it is important that they are numerous and as large as possible. It is also necessary that windows are placed at eye level, as the visual connection to the outside world is paramount. If a space only has windows above eye level it does not matter if they are large and the amount of daylight is generous, as the lack of a visual connection at eye level emphasises an inherent sense of isolation and restriction. This often causes physical discomfort as a result. The need for visual control of the experienced physical space also includes interior connections, e.g. across level differences and spatial zones or from one space to another. One must be able to see what cannot be heard.

Visual noise is an important factor and given the need for large windows and openings, the risk of visual noise increases accordingly. The issue of visual noise can be accommodated by minimising flickering and intense decorations and materials indoors as well as working consciously to establish a buffer zone between public space and private space. Consistent motion and activities are less disturbing and intrusive if they are kept at a safe distance from the user. If they are not right outside the windows in question it is easier to ignore them.

A SENSIBLE PERSPECTIVE

Living with a sensory disability implies design requirements for an accessible physical environment that include means of way finding and orientation as well as assistive technology. But if the ambition is to ensure more than mere physical access and also to open the door to the world of amazing, unforgettable and breathtaking sensory experiences of architecture and architectural quality, the concept of sensory accessibility needs to be integrated in the design process and considerations.

Working with different groups of sensory impairments shows both common denominators and mutually contradictory design requirements. Thus it is not possible to define one design solution accommodating all sensory disabilities and hence easily assuring universal sensory accessibility. We can conclude that there is no single solution to accommodate everybody's needs and physiological condition. It is necessary for architects and designers to make informed choices and priorities in the design process when including sensory disabilities and aspects as architectural parameters.

An important aspect is the significance of the interaction and synergy between architectural elements such as proportions, acoustics and connections. Many desires and requirements are concerned with the interrelation between these elements, and the proper accommodating design solution needs to grow out of the synergy of the specific spatial context and sensory impairment. As the architectural elements in question are all fundamental to any architectural design, sensory accessibility considerations must be included in the very beginning of any design process. These are not elements that can be adjusted easily or without extra cost once the building is constructed.

Besides increasing accessibility to the experiences of architectural quality, sensory accessibility also increases access to other decisive aspects of architecture, the physical setting of our lives. Sensory accessibility emphasises sociological and existential aspects of being and as such also increases the quality of life not only for people living with a sensory disability but for everyone.

We constantly sense, consciously or subconsciously, the architectural elements that separately and jointly define the qualities and character of a space. Often small nuances determine what sensory quality dominates the individual experience, but it is also the individual primary sense that defines what qualities are even perceived, and thus whether the architectural experience is sensory accessible.

REFERENCES

Hall, ET, The Hidden Dimension, Doubleday & Company, Inc, 1966, p 65

Pallasmaa, J, The Eyes of the Skin, Architecture and the Senses, Academic Group Ltd, London, 1996, p 36

Pallasmaa, J, The Eyes of the Skin, Architecture and the Senses, Academic Group Ltd, London, 1996, p 36

Karlsson, G, Living as a Blind Person, Phenomenological and Psychological Investigations, Calsson Publishing House, Stockholm, 1999, p 34

McLinden M and McAll S: Learning through Touch, David Fulton Publishers Ltd, London, 2002, p 25

Pallasmaa, J, The Eyes of the Skin, Architecture and the
Senses, Academic Group Ltd, London, 1996, p 36

Karlsson, G, Living as a Blind Person, Phenomenological
and Psychological Investigations, Calsson Publishing House,
Stockholm, 1999, p 31

Karlsson, G, Living as a Blind Person, Phenomenological
and Psychological Investigations, Calsson Publishing House,
Stockholm, 1999, p 150

Hesselgren, S, The Language of Architecture, Student Literature, Lund, 1967, p 118

Pallasmaa, J, The Eyes of the Skin, Architecture and the
Senses, Academic Group Ltd, London, 1996, p 28

Hall, ET, The Hidden Dimension, Doubleday & Company,
Inc, 1966, p 65

LITERATURE

Hall, ET, The Hidden Dimension, Doubleday & Company,
Inc, 1966

Hesselgren, S, The Language of Architecture, Student
Literature, Lund, 1967

Karlsson, G, Living as a Blind Person, Phenomenological and Psychological Investigations, Calsson Publishing
House, Stockholm, 1999

McLinden M and McAll S: Learning through Touch,
David Fulton Publishers Ltd, London, 2002

Pallasmaa, J, The Eyes of the Skin, Architecture and the

Senses, Academic Group Ltd, London, 1996

Percival, J, Hanson, J, Osipovic, D, A positive outlook? The Housing needs and aspirations of working age people with visual impairments, Disability & Society, Vol.21, No 7, December 2007, pp. 661-675

Ryhl, C, A House for the Senses, The Royal Danish Academy of Fine Arts, School of Architecture, Copenhagen, 2003

Steinfeld, E, Danford, SS, Theory as a Basis for Research on Enabling Environments. (Eds.) Enabling Environments. Measuring the Impact of Environment on Disability and Rehabilitation. Kluwer Academic/Plenum Publishing, NY, 1999

ILLUSTRATIONS

All photos in the article are by the author.

PART 3 **PRODUCT DESIGN**

John Clarkson
Onny Eikhaug
Ingrid Rønneberg Næss
and Trond Are Øritsland
Marianne Støren Berg

JOHN CLARKSON is Professor of Engineering Design in the Department of Engineering at the University of Cambridge and Director of the Cambridge Engineering Design Centre.

Following undergraduate and postgraduate degrees at Trinity Hall, Cambridge in electrical engineering John joined PA Consulting Group where he gained wide experience of product development with a particular focus on the design of medical equipment and high-integrity systems.

John later returned to the Department where his research interests are in the general area of engineering design, with particular reference to process management, change management, healthcare design and inclusive design.

DESIGNING A MORE INCLUSIVE WORLD
John Clarkson

Good design is good business. Research by the UK Design Council (2005) has shown that an index of design aware companies outperformed the FTSE All share index by over 200% in both bull and bear markets over a 10 year period. There are clearly other indicators of good business management apart from design; however, the evidence that 'good design is good business' is compelling.

Design is not optional, it is an inevitable consequence of specifying or developing a product or service. The question is whether your design is good, bad or indifferent. Good design helps to manage development risk, asking

- Are you building the right products (or services)?

- Are you building the product right?

In addition, since the cost of change increases exponentially throughout the design and development lifecycle (Mynott et al., 1994), it is imperative that the project team have a thorough understanding of the real user and business needs at the start of the design process and correctly translate these needs into an appropriate requirements specification. This is particularly relevant for Inclusive Design, where the objective is to design products and environments that are usable by all people, to the greatest extent possible, without the need for adaptation or specialised design (Mace et al., 1991).

Many exemplars of Inclusive Design exist from such companies as ErgonomiDesign (www.ergonomidesign.com), IDEO (www.ideo.com), Smart Design (www.smartdesignworld-

wide.com), Factorydesign (www.factorydesign.co.uk) and
Sprout Design (www.sproutdesign.co.uk) to name just a few.
To understand their success it is first important to under-
stand the drivers behind Inclusive Design.

AN AGEING WORLD

The demographics of the developed world are changing;
longer life expectancies and a reduced birth rate are resulting
in an increased proportion of older people within the adult
population. This is leading to a reduction in the Potential
Support Ratio (PSR), which is the number of people aged 15-
64 who could support one person aged over 65 (UN, 2004):

- In 1950 the worldwide PSR was 12:1 ;

- In 2000 the PSR was 9:1 ;

- by 2050 it will be 4:1 globally and 2:1 in the developed
  world.

Maintaining quality of life and independent living for this
ageing population is increasingly important and will soon be
an absolute necessity for all countries in both the developed
and developing world – independent living goes from being
an aspiration to an imperative.

With increasing age comes a decline in capability (Figure 1),
yet often increased wealth and free time. Where previous
generations accepted that capability loss and an inability to
use products and services came hand in hand, the baby-
boomer generation now approaching retirement are less
likely to tolerate products that they cannot use, especially if
this is due to unnecessary demands on their capabilities.

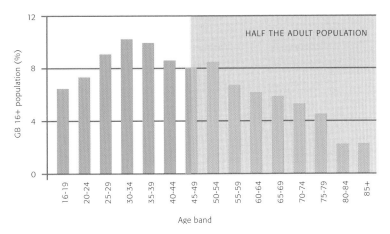

Figure 1 – Percentage of each age band in Great Britain that have less than full ability (Grundy et al., 1999)

Typically, people are viewed as being either able-bodied or disabled, with products being designed for one category or the other. In fact capability varies continuously, and in reducing the capability demands of a product, inclusive design not only helps meet the needs of those who are excluded from product use, but also improves the product experience for many others. This is consistent with research undertaken by Philips (2004) which found that two thirds of the population as a whole have difficulties with technological products (Figure 2).

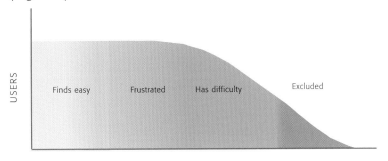

Figure 2 – Many people have difficulties with technological products (Clarkson et al., 2007)

When the capability demanded by a product exceeds that of the user, they can no longer use it. Often this is seen as the person's fault for having a poor memory, reduced strength or imperfect vision. However, inclusive design places the responsibility with product designers to ensure that the capability levels required to use a product are as low as possible.

In the UK there are approximately 60 million people, a single number that hides significant diversity of age, status and capability:

- half of all adults are aged 47 or over;
- the gender ratio is approximately 50 : 50;
- 23% are grandparents and 18% are children;
- 17% are disabled;
- 14% have arthritis and 2.5% have diabetes.

As a consequence, it is *normal* to be *different*.

INCLUSIVE DESIGN

The British Standards Institute (2005) defines Inclusive Design as "The design of mainstream products and/or services that are accessible to, and usable by, as many people as reasonably possible ... without the need for special adaptation or specialised design."

In this sense products must be:

- Functional – providing suitable features to satisfy the needs and desires of the intended users;
- Usable – providing pleasure and satisfaction in use through easy operation;
- Desirable – conferring social status, or providing a positive impact on quality of life, whilst being aesthetically striking or pleasant to use;
- Viable – assuring business success through delivery to

market at the right time and at the right price.

Any potentially inclusive product or service is developed by starting from a challenge, captured as a perceived need. Transforming this need into a solution that can successfully satisfy the real need requires an appropriate design process. There are many ways to describe this transformation, but the 'waterfall' model (figure 3) is one of the most useful:

- Discover – the systematic exploration of the perceived need to ensure the right design challenge is addressed, with due consideration of all stakeholders; leading to the first output, an understanding of the real need;

- Translate – the conversion of this understanding into a categorised, complete and well defined description of the design intent; leading to the second output, a requirements specification;

- Create – the creation of preliminary concepts that are evaluated against the requirements; leading to the third output, concepts;

- Develop – the detailed design of the final product or service, ready to be manufactured or implemented; leading to the final output, solutions.

Note that all decisions made throughout the process affect the level of design exclusion. Above all, knowledge of the intended users is particularly important.

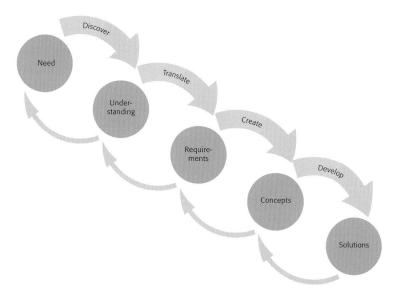

Figure 3 – An inclusive design process (Clarkson et al., 2007)

UNDERSTANDING USERS

Any interaction with a product or service typically requires a cycle where the user perceives, thinks and acts; where for the most part, perceiving requires sensory capability, thinking requires cognitive capability, and acting requires motor capability (figure 4). The interaction between a product or service and the user's capabilities is also influenced by the environment in which it is used.

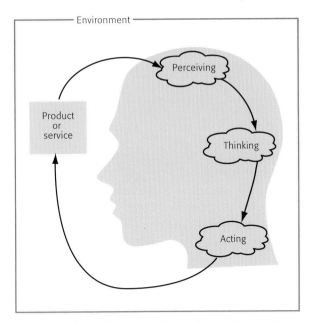

Figure 4 – The product interaction cycle (Clarkson et al., 2007)

The following seven capability categories are helpful to measure a person's capability, or assess the ability level that a product demands in order to use it (Keates and Clarkson, 2003):

- Vision is the ability to use the colour and brightness of light to detect objects, discriminate between different surfaces, or see the detail on a surface;

- Hearing is the ability to discriminate specific tones or speech from ambient noise and to tell where the sounds are coming from;

- Thinking is the ability to process information, hold attention, store and retrieve memories and select appropriate responses and actions;

- Communication is the ability to understand other people, and express oneself to others (this inevitably overlaps with vision, hearing, and thinking);

- Locomotion is the ability to move around, bend down,

climb steps, and shift the body between standing, sitting and kneeling;

- Reach & stretch is the ability to put one or both arms out in front of the body, above the head, or behind the back;

- Dexterity is the ability of one or both hands to perform fine finger manipulation, pick up and carry objects, or grasp and squeeze objects.

When designing a new product or service it is essential to ensure that the demands it makes of its users, in the intended (and possible) use environments, do not exceed their capabilities. Further, if the sensory demands result in significant levels of exclusion or difficulty, there is little value in ensuring that the cognitive and motion demands are less onerous. Similarly, if the sensory demands are moderated, but the cognitive demands are excessive, then there may be little value in easing the motion demands. Ensuring a 'balanced' set of demands may result is an iterative design process, looking at different product concepts, their interaction sequences and resultant levels of difficulty and exclusion.

The following sections provide some examples of user capability loss and the challenges these might pose to effective use of products and services. As with any descriptions of general behaviour, much is lost with regard to the specific challenges experienced by individuals, and the coping strategies that they might adopt. However, some description is better than no description, and what there is might inspire readers to learn more through interaction with real users.

SENSORY CAPABILITY

Vision capability may be characterised in a number of ways, including measures such as ocular accommodation, i.e. the ability to change the focal length of the eye. This varies dramatically with age (figure 5), ensuring that most users require some form of visual assistive technology (glasses) as they grow older. This can cause problems in the home with the use of everyday appliances and outside of the home with navigation, transportation, shopping etc.

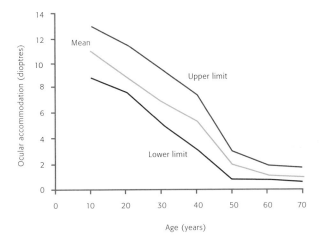

Figure 5 – Variation of ocular accommodation with age (Vasilieff and Dain (1986) © Elsevier)

A particular problem for older users is the safe administration of medication. Four in five people over 75 in the UK take at least one prescribed medicine, and 36% take four or more medicines (DH, 2001) the majority of which are administered in the form of tablets, either in bottles or in blister packs. A pharmacy label is attached to each pack, identifying the patient, medication and dosing regime. However, since all these labels look rather similar and often have poor definition, identification errors can arise for those with visual capability loss (figure 6).

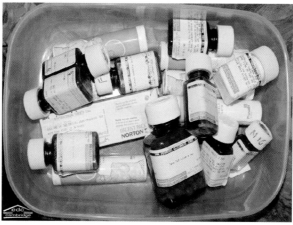

Figure 6 – The impact of moderate acuity loss on medication identification

Hearing capability may be characterised in terms of an individual's ability to distinguish and interpret sounds and speech. Again, this varies dramatically with age (figure 7), and can cause particular difficulty in understanding speech within noisy environments. It is important that sounds associated with users' interactions with products or services take account of this trend, noting that changing the tone of a signal may have a more effect than changing its volume for less able users.

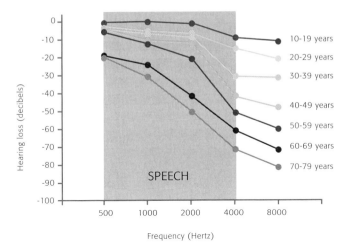

Figure 7 – Variation of hearing loss with age. Annals of Otology, Rhinology and Laryngology by Rosen S., Plester D., et al. Copyright 1962 by Annals Publishing Company. Reproduced with permission of Annals Publishing Company in the format other book via Copyright Clearance Center.

COGNITIVE CAPABILITY

Thinking, or "cognition", is the way we respond to sensory perceptions of the world, process them and choose our responses. The brain organises incoming sensory information, processes it in the light of consciousness through attention and then initiates responses in the form of actions. At a higher level, the sensory, cognitive and motor functions of thinking are integrated within the brain. Understanding the interaction between these is a basis for good product design. As with other capabilities, there is a measurable variation of performance through life (figure 8).

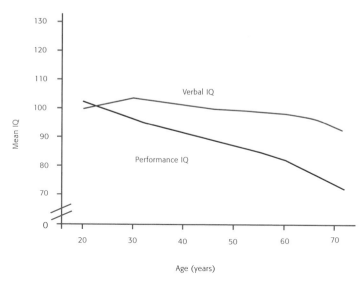

Figure 8 – Variation of cognitive capability with age. Mechanisms of Age-cognition Relations in Adulthood by Salthouse TA. Copyright 1992 by Taylor & Francis Group LLC – Books. Reproduced with permission of Taylor & Francis Group LLC – Books in the format other book via Copyright Clearance Centre.

Verbal IQ, the ability to communicate with language, is generally maintained through life, while performance IQ, the ability to process information, decreases with age. The complexity of many modern day products challenges our cognitive ability. For example, instructions for self-build furniture are a continuing source of frustration, trying with the minimum use of words – which is inclusive from a language perspective – to guide users through an often complex and unfamiliar construction sequence. Set-up sequences for many modern electronic appliances, such as digital television systems and wireless networking players, can also confound all but the most persistent users. Fortunately, some vendors recognise these difficulties and provide user-friendly installation services. Many others do not. As a result two out of three Americans have been reported as having lost interest in a technology product because it seemed too complex to set up or operate (Philips, 2004).

MOTION CAPABILITY

Motion capability may be characterised in a number of ways, including descriptions such as locomotion (waist down movement), reach and stretch (waist up movement) and dexterity (fine hand movement). All clearly have an impact on product interaction and need to be taken into account when designing products and services.

In order to move around, we require adequate muscle strength, motor control and balance. Locomotion includes the ability to sit down and stand up, to get up and down from the floor, and to move around in an environment by walking and ascending or descending steps. Reach and stretch includes the ability to reach one or both arms out from the body, either in front of and above the body (e.g. to put on a hat), or out to the sides (e.g. to reach objects while sitting at a desk). Dexterity includes the ability to grasp, move and exert forces to use and operate various products, which may need to be grasped, pushed and pulled. Both hands are often used at the same time to manipulate objects, i.e. coordinating strength and dexterity in the fingers with sensory capability and motor control.

Age-related or temporary loss can affect all of these capabilities leading to a variety of difficulties. For example, products designed for two-handed use may need to be operated with one hand, as a result of permanent (e.g. due to stroke), temporary (e.g. due to fracture) or situational capability loss (e.g. due to the need to hold onto a grip while standing on a train). This places additional demands on the design team to accommodate such behaviour.

Locomotion is fundamental to enable access to the majority of products and services. A washing machine becomes inaccessible to those without even basic (with or without assistance) locomotion capability; however, it may also remain inaccessible to those who can gain proximity to it if they are unable to bend sufficiently to load or unload the machine.

For other products gaining proximity is sufficient to afford the user an opportunity to use them.

Reach and stretch and dexterity govern access to the majority of products and services that demand some degree of motion interaction. The combination of fine hand-control with gross movement, afforded by movement of the upper limbs, enables users to exert clamping forces between fingers, to hold larger objects in the palm of the hand, and to exert pulling and pushing forces to manipulate objects. Such interactions are often subtle and rather complex, demanding careful observation to understand exactly what is taking place and how different individuals tackle the same task in different ways.

There are capability measures that show variation of performance through life. Figure 9, for example, shows the variation of mean grip strength by age, distinguishing between short-term (e.g. undoing the lid of a jar) and long-term (e.g. carrying a bag of shopping home) performance.

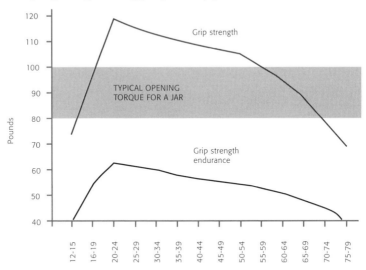

Figure 9 – Variation of grip strength with age. Journal of Applied Psychology by Burke, Tuttle et al. Copyright 1953 by American Physiological Society. Reproduced with permission of American Physiological Society in the format other book via Copyright Clearance Center.

Figure 9 also highlights the fact that jars that are too diffi-cult for children to open are also going to be too difficult for many older adults. This may have more serious consequenc-es if the 'jar' is actually a medication bottle with a child-re-sistant cap.

There has been much valuable research over the years dedi-cated to understanding the interplay between motion capabil-ities and product demands. This ranges from the provision of anthropometric data, for example, by Dreyfuss (Tilley, 2002) and the UK Department of Trade and Industry (Norris and Wilson, 1999; Peebles and Norris, 1998; Smith et al., 2000); to the provision of assessment tools, for example, HADRIAN (Marshall et al., 2001) and the exclusion calculator (Clarkson and Keates, 2004); the publication of product assessments (DTI, 2000; Ricability, 2000; Yoxall et al., 2006); and the provision of design guidance (Clarkson et al., 2007; Rica-bility, 2001). All these approaches add value to the design process, but are no substitute for involving real users in the design process (Keates, 2006).

INVOLVING USERS

The interaction between a product or service and the user's capabilities is often complex and at the same time rather sub-tle, so that the involvement of the user in product and service design is critical to the success of this process. Users may be employed in a variety of ways to maximise their influence on the understanding of the real need, in defining require-ments, and in evaluating concepts and final solutions. They may include:

- Average users – who are generally able-bodied can advise on the usability and desirability of the emerging product or service;

- Extreme users – who, by describing the impact of their severe capability loss, can often inspire creative design;

- Boundary users – who, whilst at the limit of being able to use the new product or service, advise on its accessibility;

- Expert users – who are experienced in rigorously reviewing products and services.

There are many different ways of involving users in the design process. They can be asked about their lives, what they want or need or what they think of the design. They may be observed in daily life to understand their experiences and needs. They can also participate as co-designers, providing direct input into the creative process.

Users may also be real or imaginary; whilst the involvement of real users adds particular richness to the design process, imaginary users, or personas, can provide a qualitative representation of user behaviour and bring users to life by giving them names, personalities and lifestyles. They identify the motivations, expectations, goals, capabilities, skills and attitudes of users, which are responsible for driving their product purchasing and usage behaviour. Although personas are fictitious, they are based on the knowledge of real users and may be described to suit the market segmentation adopted by an organisation.

In the absence of real or imaginary users, designers may also employ a range of other tools to gain insight into the difficulties that may arise in using products. These range from capability simulators to audit tools that predict likely levels of exclusion.

DESIGN TOOLS

Capability simulators are devices that designers can use to reduce their effective ability to interact with a product. Physical simulators can be worn to impair movement or vision, whilst software simulators modify an audio clip or photo image, so that someone who is fully able perceives the information as though he or she has a capability loss. These simulators can provide a quick and cheap method to help designers empathise with those who have capability losses, increase their understanding of the different losses, and simulate how exclusion occurs during product interaction. Their relative cheapness, speed and ease of access mean that these simulators can be used both early on and repeatedly throughout the design process (Clarkson et al., 2007).

Alternatively, an exclusion audit may be undertaken to evaluate different products or concepts by comparing what proportion of the population will be unable to use them. A task analysis is used to record the activities that are necessary to use the product, then the capability demands of these activities are assessed in terms of the levels of exclusion that result (Figure 10), allowing design decisions to be based on meaningful numbers.

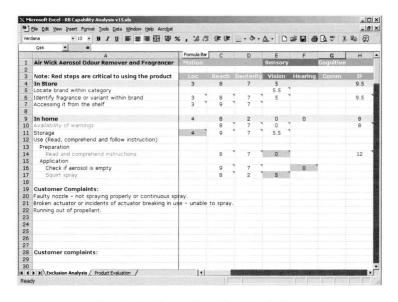

Figure 10 – A task analysis of the product life cycle (Clarkson et al., 2007)

Objective scales may also be used to measure the level of capability that a product or service demands in order to use it.

Once the appropriate demand level has been identified, data from the 1996/97 Disability Follow-up Survey (Grundy et al., 1999) can be used to estimate the number of people that will be excluded (figure 11). This in turn can highlight particular accessibility problems and corresponding opportunities for product improvement.

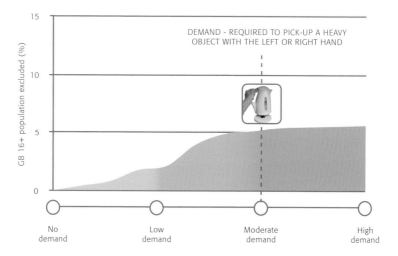

Figure 11 – Objective scales can be used to measure capability demands (Clarkson et al., 2007)

PRODUCT AND SERVICE AUDITS

A number of tools and approaches have been described that assist in auditing a new product or service. These may be used in combination (recommended) or individually. A particularly effective approach is to combine the use of user trials, expert assessment and exclusion audits to review a new product. This has the advantage that each tool looks at the product from a different perspective, leading to insights that could not be gained when using only one tool. For best results, it is necessary to aggregate rather than correlate the insights gained from using each tool (Clarkson and Keates, 2003).

Audits must also be undertaken within a framework that describes the context of use of the product and the particular activities that are to be reviewed. Task analysis may be employed to describe the activities undertaken when using a product, providing a graphical means to describe the product lifecycle of use (Figure 12); the context of use; and the user journey.

Figure 12 – A task analysis of the product life cycle (Clarkson et al., 2007). Interface for Product Inclusion Calculator by Sprout Design Ltd 2006.

The lifecycle of a kettle would describe its journey from purchase, through set-up and use to disposal; the context of use would describe its role in the making of a cup of coffee; while the user journey would describe all the activities, including those relating to other products, required to make the cup of coffee. An audit of the product lifecycle and the user journey would help to identify specific actions that might cause difficulty or exclusion, allowing any shortcomings in the kettle (or other associated products) to be identified (Keates and Clarkson, 2003).

BETTER DESIGN

The identification of potential problems with an existing design or new concept allows progress to be made towards a more inclusive solution and, by definition, an easier to use product or service. This is better design, not just inclusive design, and better design will lead to greater commercial success (Design Council, 2004). When Tesco launched their new access web-site it attracted significant levels of new business. It has since been incorporated as a set-up option in their main web-site (Figure 13).

Figure 13 – Tesco's web-site allows a choice of modes of interaction (Clarkson et al., 2007)

Inclusive, or better, design may be summarised by the challenge posed by a number of simple questions:

- Why are you starting from here?
- Is your proposition actionable?
- Are you solving the right problem?
- Are your requirements valid?
- Is your concept fit for purpose?
- Is your solution fit for purpose?

When the designers of a product or service are able to answer these questions with "as many people as reasonably possible" in mind, then it is possible to create inclusive solutions. This cannot be achieved without involving users in the process. Hence the first step towards better, or inclusive, design is to adopt a user-aware approach to all those activities that make up the design, development and delivery process.

SUMMARY

In conclusion, it is *normal* to be *different*. This places challenges on design commissioners and designers to specify and design products and services that are accessible to, and usable by, as many people as reasonably possible. Organisations that rise to this challenge will deliver better products and services that not only reduce exclusion, but also reduce difficulty and frustration to those who can already use such products and services.

Inclusive design encourages a user-aware approach, where the potential of each design decision to exclude (or include) potential customers is accepted. Good design, based on such an understanding, has the potential to delight users with usable and accessible products and services, leading ultimately to the promise of commercial success.

REFERENCES

British Standards Institute (2005). British Standard 7000-6: Design management systems – Guide to managing inclusive design. British Standards Institute, London, UK. Available from: www.bsi-global.com

Burke WE, Tuttle WW, Thompson CW, Janney CD and Weber RJ (1953) The relation of grip strength and grip-strength endurance to age. Journal of Applied Physiology, 5(10): 628-630

Clarkson PJ, Coleman R, Hosking I and Waller S (eds.) (2007) Inclusive design toolkit. University of Cambridge, Cambridge, UK. Available from: www.inclusivedesigntoolkit.com

Clarkson PJ and Keates S (2003) Digital television for all: a report on usability and accessible design – investigating the inclusivity of digital television set-top box receivers. Department of Trade and Industry, London, UK. Available from: www.digitaltelevision.gov.uk/pdf_documents/ publications/ Digital_TV_for_all_appendix_e.pdf

Clarkson PJ and Keates S (2004) Exclusion by design: an assessment of the accessibility of digital television set-top boxes. Proceedings of the 8th International Design Conference, 18-21 May, Dubrovnik, Croatia.

Design Council (2004) Design Index: the impact of design on stock market performance. The Design Council, London, UK. Available from: http://www.designcouncil.org.uk/Documents/ About design/Facts and figures/Design Index report 2005.pdf

DH (2001) National service framework for older people. Department of Health, London, UK. Available from: www. dh.gov.uk/en/Publicationsandstatistics/Publications/Publications/PublicationsPolicy AndGuidance/DH_4003066

DTI (2000) A study of the difficulties disabled people have when using everyday consumer products. Department of Trade and Industry, London, UK.

Grundy E, Ahlburg D, Ali M, Breeze E and Sloggett A (1999), Disability in Great Britain. Department of Social Security, Corporate Document Services, London, UK.

Keates S (2006) Designing for accessibility: a business guide to countering design exclusion. Lawrence Erlbaum Associates (now at Routledge), New York, NY.

Keates S and Clarkson PJ (2003) Countering design exclusion, an introduction to inclusive design. Springer-Verlag, London, UK.

Mace RL, Hardie GJ and Place JP (1991) Accessible environments: toward universal design. In Design intervention:

toward a more humane architecture, Preiser WE, Vischer JC and White ET (eds.), Van Nostrand Reinhold, New York, NY. Available from: www.design.ncsu.edu/cud/ pubs_p/docs/ ACC Environments.pdf

Marshall R, Case K, Gyi DE, Oliver R and Porter JM (2001) Supporting 'design for all' through an integrated computer aided ergonomics tool. Proceedings of the 13th International Conference on Engineering Design, 21-23 August, Glasgow, UK.

Mynott C, Smith J, Benson J, Allen D and Farish M (1994) Successful product development: Management case studies. The Design Council, London, UK. Available from: M90s Publications, DTI, Admail 528, London SW1W 8YT.

Norris B and Wilson JR (1999) Childata: the handbook of child measurements and capabilities – data for design safety. Department of Trade and Industry, London, UK.

Peebles L and Norris B (1998) Adultdata: The handbook of adult anthropometrics and strength measurements – data for design safety. Department of Trade and Industry, London, UK.

Philips (2004), The Philips Index: Calibrating the convergence of healthcare, lifestyle and technology. Philips Electronics North America, New York, NY. Available from www. designcouncil.org.uk/ Documents/About design/Design techniques/Inclusive design/Philips Index (US version).pdf

Ricability (2000) Choosing a vacuum cleaner that's easy to use. Ricability, London, UK. Available from: www.ricability. org.uk/reports/report-household/choosingavacuumcleaner/ contents.htm

Ricability (2001) Inclusive design – products that are easy for everybody to use. Ricability, London, UK. Available from:

www.ricability.org.uk/reports/report-design/inclusive design/
contents.htm

Rosen R, Bergman M, Plester D, El-Mofty A, Satti MH (1962)
Presbycusis study of a relatively noise-free population in
the Sudan. Annals of Otology, Rhinology and Laryngology,
71(Sept): 727-743

Salthouse TA (1992) Mechanisms of age-cognition relations
in adulthood. Lawrence Erlbaum Associates, Hillsdale, NJ,
USA

Smith S, Norris B and Peebles L (2000) Older Adultdata:
the handbook of measurements and capabilities of the older
adult – data for design safety. Department of Trade and Industry, London, UK.

Tilley AR and Henry Dreyfuss Associates (2002) The measure of man and woman: human factors in design. John Wiley
& Sons, New York, NY.

UN (2004) World demographic trends. United Nations Com-
mission on Population and Development, New York, NY.
Available from: www.un-ngls.org/World demographic trends
- N0463983.pdf

Vasilieff A and Dain S (1986) Bifocal wearing and VDU operation: A review and graphical analysis. Applied Ergonomics, 17(2): 86-160. Figure 5 was first published in this article
on page 83. Copyright Elsevier, 1986.

Yoxall A, Janson R, Bradbury SR, Langley J, Wearn J and
Hayes S (2006) Openability: producing design limits for consumer packaging. Packaging Technology and Science, 19(4),
pp219-225.

ONNY EIKHAUG is a Programme Leader at the Norwegian Design Council in Norway, responsible for promoting the Council's activities in the fields of people-centred design and Design for All. She is responsible for the Council's Innovation for All programme which works closely with designers and industry to introduce Design for All as an effective business tool for innovation.

She has a broad experience in international marketing, sales, innovation, product development and design management in the fields of personal products, ergonomic lighting, and contemporary furniture having worked for companies such as Unilever and Luxo across Europe and the US. She was also Managing Director of a Norwegian graphic design company. She holds an MBA from the Norwegian School of Economics and Business Administration.

DESIGN FOR ALL IN A COMMERCIAL PERSPECTIVE

Onny Eikhaug

THE NORWEGIAN DESIGN COUNCIL

The Norwegian Design Council (NDC) was established in 1963 by the Norwegian Trade Council and the Confederation of Norwegian Business and Industry (NHO). Today the NDC is organised as a foundation financed by the Ministry of Trade and Industry, through the provision of business consultancy and from its own, stand alone projects.

The ambition of the NDC is to promote design as a strategic tool for innovation, in order to offer greater competitive advantage and profitability to Norwegian trade and industry. The NDC achieves this by delivering design-related business advice to Norwegian enterprises . It disseminates its work through printed and online publication, radio, news items, web pages, exhibitions, design awards, and national and international conferences.

For several years, the NDC has emphasized the importance of Design for All whilst working with Norwegian industry. A four-year programme, named Innovation for All, was initiated to support industrial growth by contributing to and supporting new product development processes based on Design for All principles. One of the goals of this programme is to identify and demonstrate the innovation potential of this approach and to develop products and services that are user friendly and attractive for all.

A key objective of the programme is to provide relevant

knowledge of Norwegian conditions for industry and design communities, as well as offering motivating and effective approaches that can be easily adopted and implemented in everyday practice.

It is also vital to prepare Norwegian companies for forthcoming legislation that will require products and services to be more socially inclusive and cater for people with different ages and capabilities. An important part of the programme is to demonstrate the commercial as well as social benefits of this approach, emphasising Design for All as a strategic tool in user-centred innovation processes and business development.

This article is based on the research, projects and findings of the programme Innovation for All.

GLOBAL CHALLENGES

One of the challenges facing the global business community is to have a wider perspective when considering design; it is no longer a question of using design to meet purely aesthetic, functional or emotional needs. Attention has to be focused on the role design can play in promoting sustainability, enabling human rights and creating social inclusion.

Companies that can concentrate their innovation processes around understanding real consumers, respond to the new emerging trends and then meet these challenges effectively through good design practice will retain or even increase profitability and leave their competition behind (Myerson, J., 2001). In this context, Design for All can be considered a profitable strategy for innovation and an effective, low-cost, low-tech, design-driven tool that can satisfy previously unmet market demands for inclusive, mainstream products and services.

A COMMERCIAL PERSPECTIVE

The concept of 'Design for All' is founded on the principles of universal design and promotes design for human diversity, social inclusion and equality. It is an ideology that has great resonance in the current political climate where addressing exclusion is high on the agenda (Coleman, R., Harrow, D., 1997a). However, from a purely commercial perspective, it means the creation of new market opportunities and a strategy for product development and innovation that is more centred around consumer aspiration. The juxtaposition between meeting user need and working within commercial constraints can provide a space in which designers are pushed to innovate and create inventive solutions that satisfy both demands.

Companies are increasingly beholden to the perceptions of society and those companies that wish to be seen as customer-friendly, need to adopt a socially responsible approach. Design for All can help a company to achieve a position both as an attractive employer and as a key participant in the social arena. This encompasses both inclusion and sustainable development as key areas of focus and forms part of what we often term Corporate Social Responsibility.

As well as being a philosophy or ideology, Design for All is most effective as a practical approach, allowing companies to view existing customers in a new way or to expand into previously untapped markets. This is a main focus of the Innovation for All programme at the NDC.

TOWARDS A MORE INCLUSIVE SOCIETY

By identifying and presenting this innovation potential to Norwegian industry, one can induce the development of products and services that are user-friendly and attractive for all. In this context, Design for All, when adopted by industry as a strategic business tool, will become a key driver of change steering us towards a more inclusive society.

Both nationally and internationally, Norwegian companies who are not preparing for these new challenges will soon find themselves lagging behind. Whether operating in markets worldwide or meeting competition in the local marketplace, these companies will realise that global attention is directed towards human-centred issues such as sustainability and inclusion.

Design consultancies also have to pay attention as expert knowledge of, and insight into using Design for All as a strategic design tool becomes an increasingly important selling point. Individuals who realise this will have a competitive edge in the market as they can help clients to identify new potential products, services or innovations, thereby capturing a larger market with more inclusive solutions.

Therefore companies and designers who recognise these opportunities and the potential inherent in existing (and future) design challenges as a result of social, cultural and demographic changes in the market can secure future growth and profitability through unique competitive advantages and insights (Gheerawo R., Myerson J., 2006).

A SUCCESSFUL APPROACH

British retailer B&Q has taken a proactive approach to the Disability Discrimination Act 1996 (DDA) through a company-wide diversity initiative. The aim is to make B&Q stores, products, services and employment opportunities accessible to as wide a range of the population as possible, and to go beyond compliance with the DDA (Disability Discrimination Act 1996) to make Design for All a key business strategy and way of developing the B&Q brand.

The retailer has recently introduced new "inclusive" own-brand products, and more are in the pipeline. The products, a hand held sander and electric screwdriver have massively oversold and, although developed with lead groups of older users, they were deliberately marketed and designed as lifestyle tools for everyone. Recently, the products were named by a national paper in the UK as two of the 'must have' gadgets for 2005 in a list that also included Apple's iPod. (Source: Helen Hamlyn Centre, Royal College of Art)

Images: B & Q. Power to the people: Gofer screwdriver and Sandbug sander Source: The Helen Hamlyn Centre, Royal College of Art

THE OLDER CONSUMER

The ageing population in the western world is the single most important driving force behind all future design challenges.

In a few years' time, half of Norway's adult population will be over 50 years of age. Today, Norwegians over the age of 45 own more than 70 % of the population's total reserves of cash and securities. Every third krone paid out in the form of salaries goes to someone over the age of 55 years; in total, this group has more than NOK 300 billion to spend each year. And this figure is growing all the time.

Given their record-breaking purchasing power and their willingness to consume, older consumers will comprise the most potent and challenging customer group in the market in the future. Older people consume the largest share of products and services related to health or well-being as well as those involving travel services and luxury goods in Norway.

However, a new trend is emerging among these older consumers. They are remortgaging their homes in order to maintain or increase their standard of living in the latter stage of their lives – which means their heirs will not inherit houses or large amounts of money. These assets are being channelled into higher levels of consumption. Companies and design consultants who can recognise and understand the needs and purchasing power of this group will be better placed to succeed.

These customers pose also major challenges. They are not a homogenous, uniform group and can differ significantly in terms of style, preference and development. They are the most opinionated, demanding consumer group who are comfortable with consumerism but have yet to be included by mainstream design and recognised as the 'real spenders' by industry. They receive very little marketing and designers rarely accommodate their needs.

As they grow older, their sight, hearing, muscle strength, motor skills and cognitive powers will become poorer as a natural part of the ageing process (Haigh, R., 1993). Designers should therefore place an emphasis on functionality, user-friendliness and simplicity in the solutions they design without compromising the need for aesthetics, desirability or variety that may appeal to the specific emotional values that older consumers might have (Audit Commission, 2000).

NEW APPROACHES TO PRODUCT DEVELOPMENT

The concept of Design for All represents a potential for innovation that can lead to more user-friendly products and differentiate one company from another, even in a saturated marketplace. By designing products for people with reduced functional abilities, the solution arrived at will be better for all whether older or younger. Products that are easier and safer to use can be appreciated by everyone, regardless of their age or ability.

Adopting a Design for All approach places more stringent demands on a product's qualities and the way in which it functions. Thus, the method becomes an innovation tool that can be used to drive designers and manufacturers to produce unique products with improved user properties for everyone.

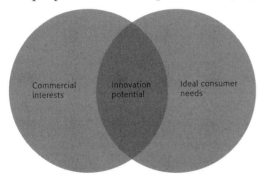

Diagram : Showing the juxtaposition between ideal consumer needs and commercial interests. Interests are overlapping when industry develops competitive advantages through Design for All and customers are offered products that better meet their needs and are barrier free. With the aging society and everyone's call for user friendly products in a complex and busy everyday life, there is increasing potential for industry applying Design for All as a strategy within user-centred innovation.

INCREASED MARKET POTENTIAL

By widening the user group for a particular product or service, companies can increase its market potential. A Design for All approach will therefore become a prominent and even preferred alternative to conventional design processes in the future.

Products aimed at a primary segment characterised by healthy and able-bodied customers, often called the average consumer, tend to exclude other groups usually on the grounds of age or ability. Design-for-All solutions include these new customer groups whilst maintaining attraction for customers within the primary segment, simply because the solution is better for everyone.

This can even increase a company's market share within the primary segment as well adding new customer groups that might not have been targeted before.

EXPAND THE MARKET POTENTIAL

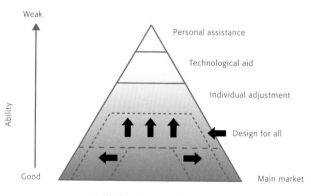

Modified - Ref. Knut Nordby 2003

The usability triangle

SIMPLIFYING DESIGN

Living as we do with busy, stressful lifestyles filled with an increasing number of technically complex products, we all have a growing need for simplification. Design for All, when embedded into the product development process, ensures that the resultant products become more simple and intuitive to use since this method also takes into account the needs of various customer groups such as older people with reduced functionality and cognitive powers and multiple minor impairments.

There are a number of other groups in society with these special needs who are currently excluded by mainstream design. These include a growing number of people with sensory impairments, physical disabilities and arthritis, as well as a large number of children.

It is not only excluded groups who benefit from simple products that are easy to use and understand. In a time characterized by a high level of self-service solutions and technological overload, everyone can benefit from simple, intuitive products. The phrase 'easy to use' or 'simple to understand' is included in almost every product design brief. Using Design for All methodologies can be a direct way of achieving this.

Some examples of simple and user friendly products

NEW LEGISLATION – NEW OPPORTUNITIES

In all markets, both nationally and internationally, more stringent legislation is being introduced to support Design for All and accessibility whilst combating discrimination and minimising exclusion.

One piece of legislation that will have a major impact on Norwegian companies is the Public Procurement Act. It stipulates that public procurers are required to choose product and service solutions that meet specific criteria in line with inclusive design criteria. Suppliers who meet these demands will be preferred.

There is also an implication for the growing number of older people related to maintaining autonomous and independent living. Enabling an older person to spend even one year longer in their homes rather than moving into care facilities can save a significant amount of money. This becomes increasingly important as there is also a decrease in the number of younger people available to support retires. There is therefore a mutual interest for both public institutions and private companies in meeting these needs in order to create a sustainable future.

However, whilst new legislation invariably involves new challenges, forward-thinking companies that can successfully embrace Design for All philosophy and practice will discover good opportunities for innovation and create competitive advantages for themselves that are in line with new legislation. Organisations that can recognise the need to move design approaches beyond mainstream markets will be best placed to capitalise on these changes in law and policy and become the preferred option in the future.

A STRATEGY FOR BETTER DESIGN

Design for All is essentially a strategy for design that centres around users. Because of this, it also represents an efficient tool for designers that deliver practical methods for developing more user-friendly products. People are a rich source of inspiration and the problems they have can give designers insights that push them to create better and more inventive design.

Companies that integrate this way of design thinking in their own strategy will obtain new expertise and insight, leading to a deeper understanding of the diversity of users with regard to age, gender, culture and level of functionality as well as individual aspirations and emotional needs.

Understanding users (consumers) also involves assessing and understanding various situations in which the product is being used. Increased knowledge of one's customers provides more information and inspiration for everyone involved in the design process, helps to challenge creativity and can lead to unexpected approaches and solutions (Warburton, N., 2003).

Thus, valuable expertise is transferred to companies, marketing consultants, designers and product developers in a way that is richer and deeper than traditional market research as it goes beyond static questioning to really understanding user need and creating empathy with their lives.

Such expertise is a valuable source of information in the wider context of business development. It can help companies to position themselves clearly in the market place, reinforce branding and give them a considerable edge over their competitors. *In this context, it becomes evident that a user-centred design process is not only a strategy to solve problems but a potent strategy for identifying problems to solve.*

Consumers themselves, especially the marginalised groups,

therefore represent a powerful tool for innovation that can have a significant influence on companies and give them the impetus to leave traditional competition behind and enter new, unexplored markets of unmet needs.

A HOLISTIC WAY OF THINKING

A Design for All strategy need not only be limited to product design, i.e. development of accessible and user-friendly products and services for as many people as possible. It can be a foundation for companies to base their entire business philosophy on. An inclusive way of thinking may impact on employment policy, personnel management and adaptation, customer service, communications strategy and marketing.

Such an approach means that the design disciplines and other areas of expertise must cooperate in providing a holistic approach that has firm roots in company policy and practice and can be implemented both at management level and throughout the organization.

It should be mentioned that practising Design for All and conducting user-centred research requires a minimum amount of investment when compared to technological research and product development. This can therefore be a low-tech, cost-saving and uncomplicated method for innovation with low barriers for implementation in both the short term and long term. It is also suitable for both small and big companies and can yield immediate results for both the company in terms of bottom line and for consumers in terms of better, more inclusive products.

Quote:
"If, for example, a company is prepared to spend 3 per cent of its turnover on technology, it might achieve the same effect through design with only 0.3 percent."
Krister Ahlström, "heavyweight industrialist"
Source: Design Matters

IMPLEMENTING DESIGN FOR ALL

How Design for All can be introduced and implemented in companies' own processes will depend on many factors and vary from company to company.

Factors of particular importance are the company's size, resources, expertise, established technology, processes and systems for product development. Experience of practical, systematic development work and design process will also be crucial.

Companies that are already experienced in using design as a tool for innovation and product development in general are more apt to successfully integrate a user centred approach in their processes. They will find this rewarding, inspiring and considerably less demanding than expected especially in terms of resource requirements, administration and coordination.

POSSIBLE LIMITATIONS

Mature design users are often larger companies that traditionally have heavy technology, with established processes and methods for product development in place that can be difficult to change.

They may find it a challenge to incorporate "user priorities" into existing processes and to engage users successfully especially at the early stages of a project. In addition, established technology and production methods may place limitations on what is possible to achieve in terms of new, user-focused solutions especially in the short term.

In such companies it is important that a user-centered focus takes into account existing frameworks and capitalizes on existing processes. It will therefore be highly important to use Design for All criteria in the decision-making process when planning for the long-term and making significant changes or investment in the company structure.

LITTLE EXPERIENCE, GREATER EFFORT

Companies with limited experience of design may find that the learning curve is steep and considerable effort is required to engage with Design for All processes. This requires more flexibility, an ability to adapt and a willingness to learn – both on the part of the company and of the designers involved in the process.

Embedding Design for All processes and user involvement in a company's own structure, technology, resources and offer will be crucial. By adapting to suit budgets, working conscientiously through problems and focusing implementation in the start-up phase, the chances of success will increase.

The scope for take-up may be increased after early successes have been proven and projects are delivered on budget, proving the cost-effectiveness of these processes. Methods and tools that have been developed in the Innovation for All programme at the NDC have been developed with the intention of simplifying processes and adapting them to the company's own capabilities and conditions.

A CONTINUOUS PROCESS

When introducing Design for All as a strategy, a number of challenges will need to be overcome that are specific to each company. The companies must therefore be self-reflective and understand their own position and aspirations in order to define the challenges that face them.

For all types of companies, regardless of size, age, resources or technological capability, it will be essential to adapt and scale a Design for All strategy that engages with existing processes and therefore impacts on their own long-term planning. Success will depend on framework conditions, implementation and their ability to maintain change. In this way, a Design for All approach should be a continuous process where everyone involved in the organization can develop along a learning curve.

CASE STUDY - USA

OXO is a successful brand whose entire product range is based on the principle of Design for All. These measuring jugs are a good example of design-driven innovation. They are the result of user involvement at an early stage and typical "low tech" product development. The resulting products are better for everyone, not just older, arthritic or disabled users.

Alex Lee, President, OXO: " Our philosophy has not only resulted in user-friendly products for a wider user group; it has also proved to be a profitable business model. We have achieved annual growth of 30 per cent since 1991 and have won more than 100 international design awards." www.oxo.com

CASE STUDY - NORWAY

The Jordan packaging project was the first pilot project in the Innovation for All programme. Jordan increased both sales and market share immediately after the launch of a new design and packaging.

"Design for All gives us a competitive edge and we have succeeded in distinguishing ourselves from our competitors," says Geir Hellerud, Product Development Manager at Jordan. (Source: Teknisk Ukeblad)

"We see very clearly the benefit of this way of thinking. We have always tested our products on consumers, but this is the first time we have taken our point of departure in elite users. We have had feedback we otherwise would not have received."

Bård Andersen, product developer

(reference is made to the article by Marianne Støren Berg, Ph.D on page 193: The Small Design Changes that Make a Big Difference – a Case Study in Packaging Design from the Norwegian Company Jordan)

CASE STUDY - JAPAN

Japan is very advanced when it comes to developing products for an ageing population and using Design for All processes. Japanese industry realized several years ago that the market for products that meet the needs of a greater diversity of customers has an enormous commercial potential. In 2003, leading Japanese companies formed the International Association for Universal Design (Universal Design is the Japanese term for Design for All). This design organization now has 144 members, including household names and global brands such as Panasonic, Mitsubishi and Toyota.

Panasonic also has a good example of how Design for All

can form the basis for new product and design development. This was a strategic decision, based on Panasonic's perception of what they needed to do in order to survive in an increasingly tough market.

Panasonic - Tilted washing machine

One result from this way of thinking was the tilted-drum washing machine. Atypically, the revolutions per minute and energy consumption were not considered the most important factors for consumers. Panasonic developed their new, energy efficient washing machine with an angled door placed at a height that makes it easier to use. The result is better use for a wider range of customers as the picture demonstrates and a unique selling point – easier loading of kilos of laundry – that differentiates this Panasonic washing machine from the competition.

INCLUSIVE MARKETING

We generally only see young, Western, beautiful, healthy people with no disabilities in advertising campaigns and in other forms of communication. However, most companies claim to target a wide diversity of customers in terms of gender, age, culture, abilities and lifestyle and do not wish to be labelled as discriminatory. This is a dichotomy between product aspiration and the realities of marketing.

Photos by Elisabeth Ohlson Wallin, for an advertising campaign promoting Design for all in Sweden 2006, by EIDD

Marks & Spencer, a UK retailer of clothing in the high street, has understood this and now uses a wider range of models in its advertising. The company realised that it was a mistake to identify 'trendy' as meaning 'young' as its solid consumer base was the over 50's who wanted fashionable, exciting products at a good price. They employed people who were identified as icons for this age group, people such as the model Twiggy and the actor Antonio Banderas. The result of this is that many more older customers feel they can identify with M&S and are part of M&S' target group. This change in attitude has had a positive effect on the company's development, growth and importance in the market.

DEFINING SUCCESS

There are a number of criteria that are essential in introducing a Design for All strategy into a company's core practice.

1. INTEGRATION AS PART OF OVERALL BUSINESS STRATEGY - ROOTED IN THE ORGANISATION

Design for all must be firmly rooted in company policy. It must be firmly rooted in both management structure and throughout the organisation itself. This includes all the departments, not just the Design department. These can include Development, Marketing, Sales, Communication, Production, Logistics and Finance.

Definite goals and operational measures that dictate the
strategy are important but it is even more essential to display
the benefits of such an approach in order to show employees
what can be achieved and persuade them to adopt it. This
can include demonstrating an increased understanding of
the market and customers, new insights from user involvement, greater innovation, better competitive edge, growth
and profitability.

By doing this the employees will engage with Design for All
whilst maintaining ownership of their own tasks and responsibility, even adapting company policy to suit their own
purpose. In this way, user-centred thinking can be secured
within the organisation across all subject areas and departments.

2. COMBINING CREATIVE DESIGN EXPERTISE AND INTERDISCIPLINARY APPROACH

Adopting an interdisciplinary approach throughout the process is vital to success. Mutual understanding and collaboration between complementary skills within an organisation is
also vital.

Various types of design expertise that focus on user priorities
must be involved from start to finish.

3. USER PARTICIPATION AND LEAD USERS

Involving users and securing the right type of users is of key
importance and must be addressed before starting. There is a
need for systems to manage and introduce user involvement
throughout the company as well as systems for user participation, the organisation of resources and continued planning
throughout the various stages of the process.

In this context, a user-centred approach means involving users who are not normally considered by mainstream design
such as older people or those with disabilities. These groups

can form the lead users in the project. The concept of lead users means people with critical needs that can challenge the functional capacity of the product and encourage the designers to think beyond their current constructs.

4. AN INCLUSIVE DESIGN APPROACH SHOULD BE ADAPTED AND TAILORED TO THE COMPANY'S OWN DEVELOPMENT PROCESS

Design for All is best implemented in the company's own product development and design process by ensuring that everyone involved, both project participants and decision-makers, define and plan the process together. A good starting-point is creating a common understanding of how - and a platform on which - Design for All can be integrated and tailored to the company's own, established process. It is important to define how user needs can be voiced and subsequently influential in design decisions and when user involvement in the remain various phases is to be implemented.

Furthermore, it is crucial that communication and criteria tools are developed that can define the project's potential and ensure that all aspects and project criteria throughout the value chain are taken into account, e.g. marketing, branding, production, price, finance, environment, logistics, distribution. The commercial basis (the customer's willingness to pay) for user-centred solutions must be demonstrated and described in order to secure and support the decisions concerning the selected Design for All solutions. Seen as a whole, this means that the Design for All aspects must be included in a holistic and financially sound approach.

IN CONCLUSION

Together, these criteria give some measure of success and, if met, can help Norwegian businesses use design in general, and Design for All in particular, to create competitive advantage and move closer to the consumer. Design for All is a powerful tool for innovating in existing markets as well as opening the door to new markets. In the consumer-driven, more socially conscious world of today, this methodology is becoming increasingly important and is something that companies cannot afford to ignore.

REFERENCES AND BIBLIOGRAPHY

Audit Commission, 2000. "Fully Equipped: The Provision of Equipment to Older or Disabled People by the NHS and Social Services in England and Wales". The Audit Commission, London.

Clarkson J, Coleman R, Keates S & Lebbon C (2003) "Inclusive Design: design for the whole population, Springer Verlag, London

Coleman, R., Harrow, D., 1997a. "A Car for All – Mobility for All". Retrieved from http://www.hhrc.rca.ac.uk/resources/publications/CarforAll/carforall1.html. Paper presented at the Institute of Mechanical Engineers, DesignAge Publications, London.

Gheerawo R., Myerson J., 2006. "Living Independently – Inspirational Kitchen and Bathroom Design for Older People" – presented at the IAUD conference in Kyoto, October 2006. The Helen Hamlyn Research Centre, Royal College of Art, Kensington Gore, London, UK, SW7 2EU

Haigh, R., 1993. "The Ageing Process: A Challenge for Design". In: Applied Ergonomics, 24, 1. Butterworth-Heinemann, London, pp 9-14.

KODE Design 2005. "Tilgjengelig emballasje. Forprosjekt. Brukerorientert nyskaping med Design for Alle som virkemiddel". (English: "Accessible packaging. User oriented innovation with Design for All as strategy"). Report within the Innovation for All programme at the Norwegian Design

Council, 01.10.2007: www.norskdesign.no, Oslo.

KODE Design 2005. "Fra barrierer til innovasjon" (English: "From barriers to innovation"). Report within the Innovation for All programme at the Norwegian Design Council, 14.06.2006: www.norskdesign.no, Oslo.

Myerson, J., 2001. "Design DK: Inclusive Design". (Reprint) Danish Design Centre, Denmark, p 5.

Warburton, N., 2003. "Everyday Inclusive Design". In: Clarkson J, Coleman R, Keates S, Lebbon C (eds.) Inclusive Design – Design for the Whole Population

INGRID RØNNEBERG NÆSS holds a MSc. in Product Design Engineering from the Norwegian University of Science and Technology. As part of her education she was an exchange student at Indian Institute of Science in Bangalore, India. For nearly three years she has worked as a consultant product designer. At the time being she is occupied with brand management.

TROND ARE ØRITSLAND is an industrial designer with a PhD in interaction design. He is an associate professor of interaction design at the department of Product design, Norwegian University of Science and Technology (NTNU). His research activities include Inclusive Design, game design, and peer-to peer technology for mobile phones. His main interest lies in safety critical operations in control rooms, and the application of embodied mind theory in design. He currently supervises three PhD students working on integrated operations in the petroleum industry.

INCLUSIVE MAINSTREAM PRODUCTS

Ingrid Rønneberg Næss and Trond Are Øritsland

INTRODUCTION

When designing for disabled people, designers tend to
design for stereotypes and emphasize function rather than
style. However, just like everyone else, disabled people wish
for products that offer functionality, dignity, enjoyment and
an attractive identity. One may say there is a divergence
between designers and users. Inclusive design has been
introduced as a tool to avoid this problem. Inclusive design
emphasizes the elimination of discrimination and maximiz-
ing products' market potential. According to its followers,
everyone can use inclusively designed products. The question is - do we want to?

In our opinion, the historical focus on usability and utility in
inclusive design has reduced the importance of what is communicated through the product's aesthetics. The aesthetics
of a product communicate something about its user's status,
emotions and values. In other words, inclusively designed
products may often disregard the essence of what makes
us human. Such products are irrelevant to larger customer
groups and stigmatizing to those who need them.

THE HISTORICAL INHERITANCE

Historically, usability and utility have dominated the philosophy of inclusive design. Inclusive design originates from
barrier free design. After World War II, therapists were able
to provide many disabled people with enough function, skills

and technology for them to live independently. However, it turned out that the surroundings needed modification and removal of barriers to become more accessible. Barrier free design solved difficulties for mobility challenged people by ramps, special lifts and bigger toilets. Yet these solutions stigmatized the users (Asmervik, 2002). The concept of universal design was introduced to challenge attitudes that barrier free design did not deal with. However, universal design was too often presented as a therapeutic intervention or as an ideological campaign. The popularity of "the Seven Principles of Universal Design" illustrates this emphasis. Moreover, the name connotes a single universal "solution" to any design problem. The concept of inclusive design was introduced to challenge the concept of universal design. Lately, inclusive design has been the trusted approach for designing desirable assistive products (Steinfeld and Tauke, 2002).

WE CREATE OUR IDENTITY

Through history the way we create our identity has changed dramatically. Formerly a person's identity was more or less predetermined. All our life we stayed in one village, the pattern of sex roles was clearly divided and our profession was inherited from generation to generation. Today society has changed. We are less defined by where we work and where we live. Our identity has become something we construct.

In 1934 the Symbolic Interactionist School in philosophy and George Herbert Mead developed the contemporary notion of social construction (Steinfeld and Tauke 2002). Mead argued that shared meaning evolved through social interaction. Hence society might be understood as a symbolic representation of that interaction. From this perspective, the relationship of material culture (products etc.) and social life is characterized by reciprocity. Material culture is a physical order that, on one hand, reflects the social order. On the other hand, material culture also prescribes a social order, and makes a social system work in specific ways. For example,

the visual appearance of automobiles will connote the differences in the status or lifestyle of their owners and contribute
to a social interaction pattern, e.g. who is attracted to whom.
Consequently, social changes are reflected by changes in the
material world, and changes in the material world contribute to the progress of social change itself. We recognize the
importance of physical objects when we construct our social
life. In other words, we use physical objects to create our
identity and place within society. One may say that people
have become products of their products.

If this is true, we realize that stigmatizing products are
particularly unfortunate for disabled people. Present assistive products often embody a "neutral" or "for all" aesthetic.
The lack of a clear aesthetic direction hinders people from
communicating their desired self through the objects associated with them. No one wants to be a product of an assistive
product.

THEORETICAL CONCEPTS FOR ANALYSIS AND DESIGN

Following Gibson (1979) our primary understanding of our
environment, our percepto-motor abilities, builds on perceptual invariants in the environment. Through evolution
and learning we develop abilities and discover how we are
able to interact with our environment. As we grow older, get
pregnant or experience some accident or illness our abilities
change – our perception and experience show a discrepancy
between what we think we can do and what we actually manage. And since our man-made environment is built to support average abilities, we are disabled.

According to Lakoff & Johnson (1980) our concepts, thinking and ideas build layer upon layer on metaphors of our
bodily experiences. Theory, ideas and social constructs stem
from our real life experiences. And so we come to semiotics,
the branch of communication theory that investigates sign

systems and the modes of representation that humans use to convey feelings, thoughts, ideas, and ideologies. For the purpose of this paper we will not discuss the various theories of the relationship between affordances, object representations and semiotics or the debates surrounding them. We propose that affordances, denotations and connotations may be applied as levels of analysis and ideation. Together they can provide a practical tool for analysing the relationship between humans' fundamental percepto-motor abilities and norms, social codes and conventions surrounding them.

The amount of meaning generated at each level may be described as follows:

- Affordances before meaning – what is it possible to use this for?
- Denotative meaning of product – what is it, what do you do with it?
- Connotative meaning of product – what does this product say about you in different social contexts? How will your using it be interpreted?

By analyzing activities and products at these three levels, a creative process can explore alternative or supplementary product functions and principle structures. Thinking in terms of affordances (and constraints) makes the designer aware of what a product does and does not allow the user to do. Thinking in terms of denotations relates products and their users to certain activities and social groups involved in these activities. Thinking in terms of connotations enables the designer to analyse the dominant feelings for types of products and activities within important social groups.

PRACTICAL APPLICATIONS
HEARING AIDS ARE NOT HEADPHONES

People with hearing impairments often use a hearing aid to enhance their hearing ability. Present hearing aids tend to be made as small and as invisible as possible. However, they are almost always visible. People without hearing difficulties also use products to enhance their listening experience. Typically they use headphones and bluetooth headsets to listen to music or to someone speaking to them on their mobile phone.

In the analysis we will find that hearing aids, headphones and bluetooth-sets are quite similar at an affordance level. All three products can somehow be placed on the head or the ear and they produce/transmit sounds. On the denotative level the products differ considerably. All three products are read as listening devices but they have different syntaxes which define their categories. The hearing aid clearly relates to assistive products because of unobtrusive colour and form. The other two products relate to consumer technology employing the opposite effects. On the connotation level the objects differ fundamentally. On one hand we have a flesh-coloured product to hide behind or in your ear. We understand that the user needs this product to listen. On the other hand we have technological fashion ornaments for trendy people. We understand that the user chooses these products to listen.

The hearing aids, headphones and bluetooth-sets are providing similar affordances, but they are denotatively and connotatively grouped apart. It seems as if assistive technology has developed a sign of its own which must be dealt with to avoid stigmatization.

A CONVENTIONAL WALKING CANE OR SPORTY TREKKING POLES

For a long time, sticks have been used as an assistive product when walking. A few years back a new product, trekking poles, emerged. Trekking poles are meant for hiking, and are used by both older and younger people. However the motivation for using them might vary. Younger people claim that the exercise will be more efficient while older people equally enjoy the fact that trekking poles help you keep your balance. Trekking poles are a good example of inclusive, mainstream design because the product has certain values and features that gives it a broader user group.

If analysed, we find that walking sticks and trekking poles are quite similar on the affordance level. You can use them to grab on to, push down on, strike at someone, et cetera. On the denotative level the products differ by height and material. The stick is an assistive product for relieving legs, while the pole is a sports product for training arms. Both products are used for assistance when walking. Connotatively, the stick relates to urban assistive products for old-fashioned, mobility challenged people. The trekking pole relates to outdoor sports activities. The poles connote people that are young at heart and enjoy the outdoors. However, the product has a limited context in which these connotations are valid. Using trekking poles in a café is unacceptable, while the stick may connote an urban sophistication that is more acceptable in the café than on a road.

NEW APPROACHES FOR INCLUSIVE DESIGN

As we grow older, get pregnant or experience some accident or illness our abilities change. Depending on our present condition, we will need different types of products to help us maintain independent living. However, we will always aspire to be associated with an identity we desire. Hence, we need inclusive, mainstream products. To design inclusive, mainstream products, we have to design highly usable products with desirable identities and features. The messages products communicate should be planned with care and emphasis. In addition, the seven principles of universal design should be fulfilled.

As we see it, assistive products can be divided in two categories. those that have to be denoted as assistive products and those that don't. For these two categories, we have developed styling and analogy approaches to designing inclusive, mainstream products. Through these approaches one designs for lifestyle rather than disability.

ANALOGY APPROACH – FOR "SECRET" ASSISTIVE PRODUCTS

The idea is to design mainstream products that fulfill needs of both able-bodied and disabled people. The product should discreetly adapt to special needs among disabled people. When using the analogy approach, one tries to uncover similar needs among able-bodied and disabled users. The needs are tangled into one mainstream product with features that are usable/ understandable for everyone (at the affordance and the denotation level), but with an identity adapted to its target group only (at the connotative level). It is worth noting that analogy-designed products do not have to fulfil exactly the same needs among able-bodied and disabled users (e.g. the trekking pole example).

By creative analogies and thinking in terms of affordances the designer will be aware of what a product does and does not allow a user to do. The clue is to design products' features in a flexible and inclusive way. Even more important is to design products' identities in such a convincing way that the assistive qualities are of secondary importance to users. In this way we achieve mainstream products which also happen to be assistive products. Hence, the analogy approach strives for the mass market and thus enlarges products' market potential dramatically. Everyone can use analogy- designed products. And everyone who identifies with the identity and desires the features wants to use the products. In our opinion, this is the only way to design truly inclusive products.

STYLING APPROACH – FOR STYLISH ASSISTIVE PRODUCTS

When intending to design an inclusive, mainstream product, one should always aspire to use the analogy approach. However, if an overt assistive-product-denotation is clearly acceptable, one should choose the styling approach. Sometimes assistive products with a clear denotation may be helpful. For example, a blind person with a blind cane, which clearly denotes an assistive product, makes it easy to arrange for this person's special needs. In such cases, one should make use of the styling approach.

When styling assistive products, desirable values and features may be added so that a styled assistive product connotes the user's lifestyle and personality. However, through the styling approach, the mass market will never be reached. This is simply due to different needs among disabled and able-bodied persons, e.g. able-bodied persons do not need a wheelchair or crutches. What one achieves through styling is a clear connection between mainstream products and assistive products. They are linked through semantic signs, and thus connote similar messages.

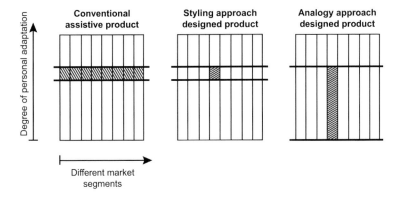

Fig 1, Styling- and analogy- approach: Conventional assistive products tend to emphasize function rather than style. These products may fulfil functional needs among a large group of disabled people, but most people find them stigmatizing. In contrast styling- and analogy designed products put an emphasis on a desirable product identity for its users. Through a styling approach disabled people are allowed to be associated with mainstream people. A person using a styled assistive product signifies she is in control of constructing her social identity, and hence she is in touch with the mainstream of society. Through an analogy approach disabled people are allowed to be interpreted as mainstream people. Analogy designed products are seen as ordinary mainstream products, but in fact they are secret assistive products. Moreover analogy designed products open up a huge market potential. The target group is everyone who shares the identity and desires the features. In our opinion, the analogy approach is the only way to design truly inclusive products.

EXAMPLE - WOMEN'S WINTER FASHION ACCESSORY FOR SHOES

For further exploration of the analogy approach, a practical case dealing with studded rubber soles has been carried through. Most people have difficulties when walking on icy surfaces. Studded rubber soles give extra friction on such surfaces. Hence, they ought to be helpful for everyone having trouble walking on slippery ice. However, it turns out that few people (even old people) are willing to use studded rubber soles due to the common perception of studded rubber soles as old people's accessories. Our purpose was to offer added friction to a wider group of the population. Since similar needs existed among able-bodied and disabled users and a clear denotation as assistive products was not desirable, we made use of the analogy approach. The solution was to make people categorise the product in a new way, namely as jewellery to put on shoes. The "shoe jewellery" identity is planned with care and emphasis to become an up-to date fashion accessory for shoes. Even if the anti-slip and inclusive qualities offered are excellent, the assistive qualities are of secondary importance to users.

CONCLUSION

The challenge of inclusive design is to move from looking merely at users, products and tasks, towards a more holistic view of how people use products to socially construct their reality. To achieve this, one has to aim for designing products that fulfil needs of both able and disabled people at the affordance and the denotation level. At the connotative level the product should communicate the desired identity of the target group.

The goal can be achieved by designing mainstream inclusive products using either a styling or an analogy approach. Through a styling approach disabled people are allowed to be associated with mainstream people. A person using a styled assistive product signifies she is in control of constructing her social identity, and hence she is in touch with the mainstream of society. Through an analogy approach disabled people are allowed to be interpreted as mainstream people. Analogy designed products are seen as ordinary mainstream products, but in fact they are secret assistive products. In our opinion, an analogy approach is the only way to design truly inclusive products.

REFERENCES

Asmervik, S (2002). Cities, Buildings and Parks for Everyone, a Universal Design Compendium. Oslo, N: Universal design – 17 ways of thinking and teaching, Husbanken.

Gibson, J J (1979). The Ecological Approach to Visual Perception. London, UK; Hougthon Mifflin Company.

Lakoff, G & Johnson, M (1980). Metaphors we live by. Chicago, US: Univ. of Chicago Press.

Steinfeld, E and Tauke, B (2002). Universal Designing. Oslo, N: Universal design – 17 ways of thinking and teaching, Husbanken.

MARIANNE STØREN BERG holds a PhD in design processes. She is practising in a series of design projects in KODE Design for companies such as HÅG, Jordan, Nera, and Stokke Varièr. She has developed the philosophy and methods of KODE Design, founded in design research. Marianne has for many years been an adviser within human-centered design for the Norwegian Design Council and has been central in establishing their program Innovation for All. She has several times served on the jury of Merket for god design within Design for All and is a frequent lecturer and workshop facilitator within Design for All and Design Management.

THE SMALL DESIGN CHANGES THAT MAKE A BIG DIFFERENCE – A CASE STUDY IN PACKAGING DESIGN FROM THE NORWEGIAN COMPANY JORDAN

Marianne Støren Berg

BACKGROUND

As consultants to many companies from various industries, our experience at KODE Design is that user priorities may be challenging to manage in design projects. Companies experience obstacles when implementing user friendly solutions. Conflicting requirements and anticipated cost consequences make decisions difficult in a design project. As the obstacles may be real or based on prejudice, there is a need for *Design for All* approaches that provide decision tools for balancing design priorities beyond the user dimension.

A pilot project concerning packaging that was carried out as part of the Norwegian Design Council's *Innovation for All* programme shows how small features in design can significantly improve the usability of the packaging when the *Design for All* approach accounts for all aspects of design.

This article reviews the process and results of a pilot project and discusses the following themes: 1) how disabled users were involved, 2) the application of a tool for securing Design for All priorities in design decisions, and 3) collaboration between Design for All experts and the rest of the project team. The article is based on one presented at the 2nd International Conference for Universal Design in Kyoto 2006.

INTRODUCTION AND BACKGROUND

Increasing emphasis has been put on investigating the implementation of Design for All (or inclusive design) in industry (Keates et al., 2000; Dong et al., 2002; Vanderheiden and Tobias, 2000). In this context, research has been conducted regarding the barriers to implementation (Dong, Keates, and Clarkson, 2003), the factors that encourage its adoption, and the approaches that lead to successful implementation.

Initial research in the *Innovation for All* programme at the Norwegian Design Council, a programme to promote innovation through Design for All in Norwegian industry, included a brief review of state-of-the-art Design for All methods and their application. The following characteristics were identified as important for implementation of Design for All approaches in industry:

- promotion of Design for All as the means for user-centred innovation
- customization of approach to industry, company, and project-specific aspects
- scaling the approach and user research according to company budgets and design tasks
- collaboration with Design for All practitioners (designers with experience of user diversity research)
- handling both *reduction* of barriers and the *formulation of value propositions* in combination

An approach should also be accompanied by good examples - showcases of Design for All. The Design for All approach that has been developed through the programme by KODE Design has focused on these identified characteristics.

Successful implementation of Design for All in Norwegian industry is an objective of the *Innovation for All* programme at the Norwegian Design Council, i.e. best practice and its implementation are central in the programme. The Innovation for All programme administered by the Norwegian Design Council is part of the Norwegian Government's Action Plan for increased accessibility for people with disabilities, the only part of the plan that is directed towards industry and the development of everyday products. Research conducted in the programme identified packaging as one area where all citizens experience barriers (KODE Design, 2005). The pilot project reported in this paper explores the implementation of a Design for All approach for the development of packaging. The project was carried out in collaboration with Jordan, a Norwegian company.

THE DESIGN FOR ALL APPROACH

In addition to improving packaging as regards usability and user experience, the aim of the project was to explore the Design for All approach that is developed within the Innovation for All programme. The approach included three central elements: 1) involving users with disabilities as lead users, 2) providing a tool for design decisions accounting for all aspects of design, and 3) a workshop procedure to integrate the Design for All approach with the existing project process at the company. These three elements are included in the process of designing new packaging for Jordan, summarized in the following steps:

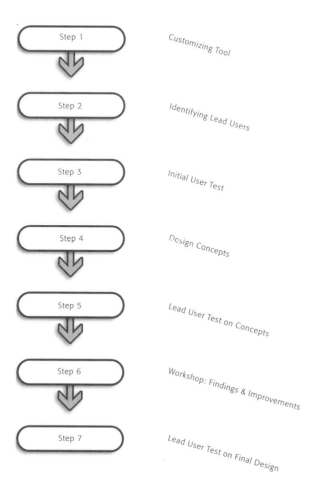

Figure 1. *The steps in the Design for All approach applied to the pilot project at Jordan.*

STEP 1: CUSTOMIZING TOOL: IDENTIFYING CRITICAL FACTORS

The project started with a workshop involving all project participants. The critical factors for all user aspects of the packaging were identified. Together the criteria formed a tool that was used throughout the project for defining the focus of the design process, for evaluating solutions and decision making.

STEP 2: IDENTIFYING RELEVANT LEAD USERS FOR THE PROJECT

The next step was to identify the relevant lead users for this project. The following users were chosen:

2 persons with arthritis

3 elderly

2 visually impaired

2 children (6 and 9 years)

2 persons without capability losses

The lead users were chosen according to how they could inform different aspects of the product.

STEP 2
Elderly people were identified as relevant lead-users to challenge packaging.

STEP 3: INITIAL USER TEST: IDENTIFYING BARRIERS AND EXPLORING PACKAGING SOLUTIONS

We tested existing toothbrush packaging, from both Jordan and its competitors, with the lead users. The user test applied all the criteria of the criteria tool, and showed us who experienced barriers with the existing design and what aspects could be improved. Based on this the project group could decide its focus for the design of new packaging.

In addition to testing existing packaging, 70 unrelated packaging solutions were explored with the lead users. What solutions facilitate intuitive opening? Which are easy to open and which are not? What graphics give great readability? – all these questions were asked during testing. The results gave us insight into good and bad packaging solutions.

STEP 3
Testing the packaging of 70 unrelated products gave us insight into a vocabulary of good and bad solutions.

STEP 4: DESIGNING CONCEPTS

This prepared the design team to start generating ideas for a new and more user friendly packaging. The team searched for solutions that would solve the evident barriers that were identified in the initial user test and for improved solutions according to all the criteria we had defined. A series of concepts were generated and models were made for concept validation by the lead users.

STEP 4
Different concepts were generated to explore solutions and directions to overcome diverse user barriers.

STEP 5: LEAD USER TESTING OF CONCEPTS

We met with the same lead users again, and tested the selected concepts in the same manner as the existing packaging. Feeding the results into the criteria tool, we could evaluate if the concepts represented improved solutions for the different users. On this basis, we refined the solutions into one concept.

STEP 5
Mock-ups of the new packaging concepts were tested by lead-users.

STEP 6: WORKSHOP: PRESENTATION OF USER FINDINGS AND CONCEPT WITH IMPROVED SOLUTIONS

The design team that had worked with the Design for All concept met with the rest of the project team in a new workshop. The recommended concept was presented, as were the different findings from the lead user testing. We had documented the testing with video and photos, and presented detailed knowledge of the users' experience with different solutions to the whole project team at Jordan.

STEP 7: JORDAN PROJECT GROUP FINALIZE PACKAGING DESIGN. LEAD USER TESTING OF NEW PACKAGING

Jordan finalized the development of the packaging. The first packaging samples from production were tested with the lead users again, to evaluate if the design had achieved the goal of being a better solution for all users. The results are discussed later in the article.

LEAD USER INVOLVEMENT

For the approach chosen in this project, user involvement is not merely about reducing barriers for the actual user group represented in the user research: they are involved as lead users. The concept of lead users, which originated in Eric von Hippel's work (von Hippel, 1986), is extreme users with critical needs who benefit significantly from solutions that meet these needs. They challenge the functional capacity of the product, in this case, the packaging.

LEAD USERS FOR SPORT EQUIPMENT - THEY ARE DIVERS FOR INNOVATION IN THE INDUSTRY

When the sports equipment industry is designing innovative skis, a father of four children on vacation can provide little input towards developing innovative performance. The industry collaborates with professional skiers who challenge the equipment. They are so-called lead users.

Figure 2.1 Lead users as a tool for innovation in sports equipment and everyday products.

LEAD USERS FOR EVERYDAY PRODUCTS - PERSONS WITH DISABILITIES CAN TRIGGER INNOVATION

People with reduced abilities challenge the performance of everyday products. They can help to identify potentials for improvements in the product, and inform the design process in various ways challenging the designers to create better solutions. If a post office is easy to navigate for a blind person, it also will be for everyone else.

Figure 2.2 Lead users as a tool for innovation in sports equipment and everyday products.

The user research was planned so that the different users were involved to extend the range of obvious barriers experienced in the packaging. The users with vision impairment, for example, evaluated brand visibility on the shelf in addition to more inevitable matters such as the readability of information and graphics. Figure 3 shows examples of how lead users informed the design process.

Selecting the profile of the lead users was central in the research design. The obvious lead users when looking at openability and handling of the packaging are people with capability losses in the hand function such as arthritis. The main reasons for the lead user profiles are listed below:

- *Users with arthritis:* openability and handling.

- *Vision impaired users:* readability of product, packaging, information and graphics

- *The elderly:* since many elderly have general reduction of capabilities they can challenge all features of the product

- *Children* have not fully developed their motor skills and thus can inform about the design of openability and handling. They are also good judges of how intuitive solutions are because they lack experience with packaging.

- *Users without capability losses:* they are not involved as lead users, but are to compare the findings from the lead users against the user experiences of the large user group without disabilities. They can indicate how important the barriers and solutions are for users with less critical needs. Do the various features of the packing create or strengthen a sales argument, do they improve the overall product experience, or do they represent a barrier and a source of irritation for all?

IDENTIFYING BARRIERS: EXITING PACKAGING PROVE FROM IRRITATING TO REPRESENTING A RISK FOR ACCIDENTS, WHEN OBSERVING THE DIFFERENT LEAD USERS.

Figure 3.1. Examples of how lead users informed the design process in the design of packaging.

OBSERVATION OF VISION IMPAIRED USER SHOWED HOW VISUALLY STRONG THE PACKAGING IS ON THE SHELF, IF IT STANDS OUT FROM THE COMPETITORS, AND HOW QUICKLY ONE SEES THE CRITERIA FOR SELECTING A TOOTHBRUSH.

Figure 3.2. Examples of how lead users informed the design process in the design of packaging.

The profile of the users, regarding the type and degree of capability impairment, was specified on the basis of their ability to carry out everyday tasks, and not on diagnostic measures. They were recruited through their interest organizations, through discussion with a contact person in the organization. We specified users who are on the borderline of managing everyday tasks independently: people who find it challenging but not impossible to handle packaging.

The users that were recruited were to some degree the result of who was available at the time. No formal recruitment procedure was followed. There was some difficulty recruiting the elderly, as the senior organization did not have systems to contact their members. For this project they were recruited through a senior centre. Formal procedures for user recruitment are called for in later projects. Finding the user is time consuming and may be a major barrier against user involvement in design projects.

When working with users with a great variation in capabilities, the research setup had to be customized to each user, and it was necessary to consciously arrange the research so that it was barrier-free. For example, the elderly found it troublesome to travel to a laboratory for focus group discussions. Observation and oral communication are better suited for most users than filling in questionnaires or technology-based research methods. The research arrangement was designed for each user group, emphasizing different aspects of the packaging and customizing interview guides and observation schemes.

In qualitative studies, such as the user research of this project, the personality of the user is also of relevance. For some aspects of the research, users who are motivated and conscious of the way they interact with the packaging are of greater value than users that are unengaged. This is of less relevance for aspects where observation techniques are used.

DESIGN FOR ALL CRITERIA TOOL

Design always involves contradictory needs and is thus a creative pursuit for generating solutions to overcome the contradictions or balance them well. The same applies for Design for All solutions. Solutions that fail to meet requirements or do not display added value and commercial potential in relation to cost are not likely to be implemented. A criteria tool provided a framework for a systematic decision-making process and formulating value propositions based on Design for All priorities.

A general tool for packaging was designed based on earlier pilot projects within Design for All at the Norwegian Design Council (KODE Design, 2003 and KODE Design, 2004) and a similar approach applied to packaging (Gough, 2004). There were two sets of criteria: those concerning the user experience, and other critical factors, such as investment level, unit cost, and logistical requirements. This tool comprised the starting point for the project, and was customized to the company and the particular project.

The main objective of the tool is to create a common understanding and common language for the user experience aspects of the packaging. Using this criteria tool, a systematic discussion was maintained throughout the design process, to secure Design for All priorities in decisions. It clearly visualized where barriers can be removed, where there is potential for improvement, or which aspects have the potential to develop added value. Each criterion is evaluated on a scale from 'impossible with urgent need for improvement' to 'very good user experience and little potential for innovation'. Differences between user groups are also displayed and indicate what commercial potential exists if various aspects are improved.

The tool was used to evaluate existing packaging solutions, to form a foundation for the project and to define the focus of the subsequent process. The most critical barrier was linked to the handling of the packaging. Both understanding how to open and actually opening the pack proved challenging. Poor openability had already been identified by the company from customer complaints. The new finding at this stage was the problems that users had in understanding just how the packaging was supposed to be opened. The users applied many different strategies to open the pack. Investigation of 70 different packaging solutions showed how openability improves when the user understands how to open the product. If the opening mechanism is intuitive, many manage to open the packaging. Of course this does not apply to everyone if the opening mechanism requires strength and dexterity. It also showed that the silhouette of the packaging is a very strong communicator, in fact stronger than graphic communication. The most effective design solution for an intuitive opening mechanism was a combination of silhouette and a strong graphical contrast element. The graphical element does not have to be illustrative nor does the differentiation need to be very "loud" to make the opening intuitive (Figure 4).

DIFFICULT TO UNDERSTAND OPENING CONCEPT

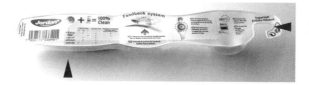

Some users try to tear here

The opening is on the back of the packaging

EASY TO UNDERSTAND OPENING CONCEPT

A sharper corner and a black arrow is all that is needed for all users to open the packaging with the anticipated opening strategy. The opening mechanism is designed to be intuitive.

Figure 4. Examples of packaging solutions that score differently regarding intuitive opening.

Figure 5 illustrates how two of the criteria were applied in the pilot project. After customizing the tool, it was used to evaluate packaging solutions throughout the process. First, it evaluated existing packaging. In the process the Design for All team applied it to evaluate ideas. And second, the proposed concept was tested and evaluated. Comparing the criteria indicates the improvement of the new solutions, and shows if the new solution matches the aspects of existing packaging that already perform well.

CUSTOMIZATION

Tow of the criteria in the general criteria tool for packaging are defined here:
Clues to open is defined as intuitive, familiar, communicative shape, and graphic information that makes it easy to sense and understand how the packaging can be opened. Open refers to how easy it is to open the pack: requires little strength and motor skills and allows flexibility concerning ways to open.

The criteria were discussed and defined according to the project.

INITIAL LEAD USER TESTING: IDENTIFIED BARRIERS

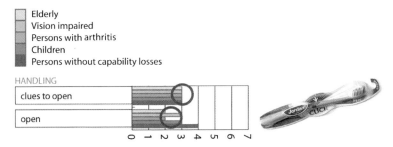

Understanding how to open and actually opening the packaging represented barriers for all users. It was an obvious issue to focus on in the further design process; a barrier shared by all.

DECIDING SOLUTIONS AND MEASURING IMPROVEMENT

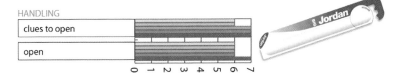

Testing of the Design for All concept showed considerable improvement compared to the exsisting packaging. It is a possibility for adding value and improving user experience.

Figure 5. Examples of the use of the criteria tool in the project: 1) customizing and specifying critical factors for the packaging, 2) evaluating existing solutions, and 3) evaluating concepts.

The criteria tool also held criteria for extending usability aspects, for example graphical design and branding aspects. Changing the opening mechanism and how the method of opening is communicated had also been taken into the graphical design concept and strengthened the design goals for the concept. When generating new solutions to improve the packaging, systematic consideration of different features was carried out. Finding solutions was a balancing act in which involvement was essential to find the line between inclusive and exclusive solutions (Figure 6).

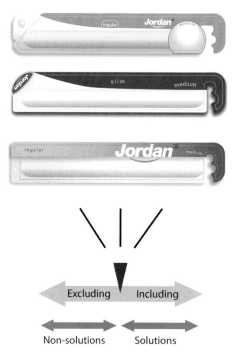

The art of Design for All lies in finding the fine balance between excluding and inclusive for most.

Packaging is a product with multifaceted functionality; protecting and stabilizing product in transport; presenting an attractive and hygienic product for sale, providing information, and producing minimal garbage. There are many conflicting requirements. A good Design for All solution is one that overcomes or balance these.

Figure 6. There is a fine line between intuitive solutions and solutions where you have to search for the opening.

COLLABORATION IN THE PROJECT

Integration is a success factor for product development. In this context, that means integration of the various aspects of product development through collaboration between the participants involved in decision making. The pilot project included two collaborative workshops with the Design for All team and the rest of the project team.

The objective of the first workshop was to customize and establish the criteria tool. The discussions and formulation of customized criteria for the project also defined the design brief and thoroughly informed the Design for All team of the agendas for the project. The second workshop aimed to report the Design for All findings and collaborate to implement these in the packaging design. It proved to be impractical for other external design partners to participate in the workshops.

The outcome of the project was Design for All concepts with recommendations for the further development of the packaging, concerning all features actually as the user experienced them. In the further development, many of the recommendations were implemented in the design, some were adjusted, resulting in less improvement, and some were left out. The pilot project generated some questions: Were the workshops important for the solutions that were implemented in the design? And would even more have been implemented if all the design partners had worked more closely together? One pilot project does not provide the answer and a question for further research is how collaboration affects the implementation of Design for All solutions.

The company reported that the most important reasons for including a Design for All approach in the development of packaging were:

- Flexibility and customization of the running project
- Explicit priorities through the criteria tool
- Scaling the research activities (The company is less willing to invest in packaging than in the product. The pilot project was at an appropriate level.)

- As a method for innovation, the Design for All approach suits their design philosophy.

DESIGN FOR ALL RECOMMENDATIONS AN PROJECT RESULTS

The Jordan project team in collaboration with their graphic design team finalized the packaging design using the Design for all concept and detailed recommendations and insights from the user testing. The first production samples of the packaging were tested with the lead users. Figure 7 shows how the final packaging design was evaluated by the lead users.

LEAD USER EVALUATION OF NEW PACKAGING

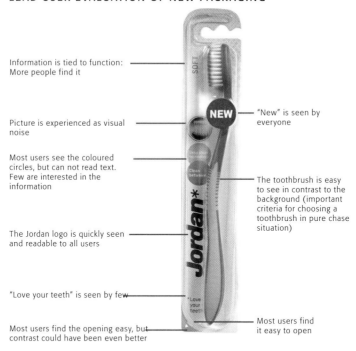

Figure 7. The packaging was designed on the basis of recommendations derived from earlier lead user testing. This reports some of the results from the testing of the final packaging.

The results from the final testing were fed into the criteria tool and compared with the results from the old packaging. Figure 8 presents the comparison and demonstrates to what degree the design has improved for the user.

LEAD USER EVALUATION - EXISTING PACKAGING

Focus areas to improve

1) Visibility criteria for purchase

2) Intuitive opening

3) Openability

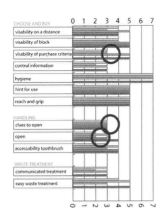

LEAD USER EVALUATION - NEW PACKAGING

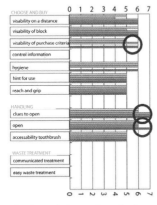

Figure 8. The criteria tool shows that the focus areas for design identified initially in the project, marked with red circles in the criteria tool, were improved for most users. These were pack recognisability (including various buying criteria), intuitive opening, and ease of opening.

211

The critical areas that represented barriers were improved for most users, but still have potential to become even better. There are still graphics and text with poor readability, but most users found this information uninteresting. The criteria the customers chose toothbrushes by, such as the brand, the size of the grip and the brush, and the softness of the brush were easier to find and read on the packaging. This was an important objective for Jordan in the project, and sales figures have proved very good after the launch of the product.

CONCLUSION

In this project, Design for All was not on the agenda initially but was introduced in the process after the product was developed and a rough design concept for the packaging existed. Like many design projects in packaging, technology was set initially which restricted solutions to meet constraints tied to this technology. This project proved that it was possible to improve the packaging in the most critical areas, even with the tight constraints of technology, logistics, unit cost, and contradictory design requirements.

The design of products and packaging involves many compromises. A Design for All approach does not change this. There are few cases where one is free to create the perfect packaging for everyone. Thus Design for All is about balancing, compromising and bridging conflicting requirements. It is about finding the small changes that make a difference for many people, and it is about creative ways of combining barrier reduction with added value in the packaging by simple means. The removal of barriers is accompanied by a value proposition.

Exploration of the Design for All approach applied in this pilot project indicates that the combination of a criteria tool for managing different packaging features and lead user involvement is a strong combination, yielding solutions that will be implemented in the design and improving the packaging usability. How the collaboration effect functions in the implementation of Design for All solutions is something that is recommended for further research.

The Design for All approach described and discussed in this paper will be revised using the findings from the pilot project. The main findings were:

- Need for improved procedures for user recruitment
- Avoid barriers in user research; customize research setup to users
- Need for further investigation of collaboration in Design for All projects

Future work will include a second pilot project before the approach is applied in up to six other projects as part of the *Innovation for All programme.*

FURTHER READING

Further reading about this project and the Design for All approach reported in this article can be found in a series of publications in the Innovation for All programme (KODE Design, 2003, 2004, and 2005). The report "Accessible packaging" (KODE Design, 2005) reports more detailed findings from the general testing of packaging in this project. An online guide presenting the Design for All approach can be found at http://veilederen.norskdesign.no/.

ACKNOWLEDGEMENTS

This chapter is based on a paper presented at the 2nd International Conference of Universal Design in Kyoto 2006. The paper was honoured at the conference as "excellent".

We would like to thank Jordan AS for providing a suitable pilot project. Particular thanks go to Onny Eikhaug for establishing and coordinating the pilot project and to Vil-helm Lange Larssen and the Norwegian Design Council for providing for design research and user-centred innovation.

REFERENCES

Dong H., Keates S., Clarkson, P.J. 2003. "Inclusive design in industry: comparing the UK and US approaches". Proceedings of INCLUDE 2003, 10:406-10:409, London.

Dong, H., Keates, S., Clarkson, P.J., and Cassim, J. 2002. "Implementing inclusive design: the discrepancy between theory and practice". Paper presented to the 7th ERCIM Workshop "User Interface for All", Paris, 24-25th Oct.

Gough, K. 2004. "On a plate: making food packaging easier to use". I-design programme publication, Helen Hamlyn Research Centre 14.06.2006: www.hhrc.rca.ac.uk/research/i-design2/kg.html, London.

Keates, S., Lebbon, C., and Clarkson, P.J. 2000. "Investigating industry attitudes to Universal Design". Proceedings of RESNA 2000, Orlando, Florida.

KODE Design 2005. "Tilgjengelig emballasje. Forprosjekt. Brukerorientert nyskaping med Design for Alle som virkemiddel". (English: "Accessible packaging. Pre-project. User oriented innovation with Design for All as strategy"). Report within the Innovation for All programme at the Norwegian Design Council, 01.10.2007: www.norskdesign.no, Oslo.

KODE Design 2005. "Fra barrierer til innovasjon" (English: "From barriers to innovation"). Report within the Innovation for All programme at the Norwegian Design Council, 14.06.2006: www.norskdesign.no, Oslo.

KODE Design 2004. "Produktvisjoner for nye inkluderende

køsystemer" (English: "Product visions for inclusive queuing systems"). Project report for the Norwegian Design Council and IT Funk, 14.06.2006: www.norskdesign.no, Oslo.

KODE Design 2003. "Å navigere uten syn" (English: "To navigate without vision"). Project report for the Norwegian Design Councils, 14.06.2006: www.norskdesign.no, Oslo.

Vanderheiden, G. and Tobias, J. 2000. "Universal design of consumer products: current industry practice and perceptions". 14.06.2006: http://trace.wisc.edu/docs/ud_consumer_products_hfes2000/index.htm

von Hippel, Eric (1986) "Lead Users: A Source of Novel Product Concepts," Management Science 32, no. 7 (July):791-805.

PART 4 **SERVICES**

Walter Mellors
Kristin Skeide Fuglerud
Bjørn Hestnes,
Peter Brooks and
Svein Heiestad

WALTER MELLORS is a Chartered Electrical Engineer, a Fellow of the Institute of Acoustics and a Member of the Institution of Engineering and Technology. For many years he was in charge of the telephone laboratory of GEC and worked with BT on the Human Factors of telephone systems. Since his retirement he has worked within ETSI on standards connected with telephony, hearing impairment, speech transmission and human factors.

wjmellors@btconnect.com

DESIGN FOR ALL IN ICT
Walter Mellors

INTRODUCTION

Europe is undergoing an information revolution that is changing the way companies do business and the way in which its citizens obtain the goods and services that they need. These changes are making telecommunications and Information and Communications Technology (ICT) an essential part of the economic, educational and social life of all. As the broadband world spreads, Telecommunications and Information Technology are converging and new technology offers unprecedented opportunities for modernisation throughout society. Unfortunately, this trend is a two edged sword in that it can exclude elderly and disabled people by failing to take their needs into account. Furthermore, as the Telecommunications and the Information Technology industries converge, the products on offer become more complex and feature rich, and the need to ensure they are easy to use becomes increasingly important and challenging to the designer.

In Europe today, people are living longer than in the past and so the population is ageing and the number of people with impairments and disabilities is increasing. It has been noted that the requirements of ICT devices have tended to exclude this growing population who suffer from age related impairments and disabilities. There is a growing recognition of the need to keep these older people and people with disabilities in active touch with society to enable them to remain independent for as long as possible. ICT can play an important part in this process. Access by elderly and disabled people to mainstream technology and technology-based services has become a major issue in enabling and facilitating their integration into the new Information Society.

As government services and important public information become increasingly available on-line, ensuring access to this information for all citizens becomes as important as ensuring access to public buildings. Achieving this accessibility requires the integration of all users into the information society, i.e. the inclusion of older people, people with disabilities and also people placed in impairing environments. This will only come about as a result of designing mainstream products and services to be accessible by as broad a range of users as possible. This approach is termed "Design for All".

Furthermore, under pressure of cost reduction, there is a growing tendency towards automation of many activities and, for example, many ticket machines and entry barriers are today unmanned. This can create increasing problems for disabled users, whose rights to participate in the normal activities of society should not be denied by the lack of required manual assistance. In general, disabled users should not be barred from equal access by the growing dependence on ICT in many areas of life. For example, any use of electronic voting should not prejudice a disabled person's right to vote.

Motivated by the changing market and also to some extent by the trend towards regulatory requirements, parts of the European ICT industry are trying to develop solutions to make their products suitable for all users, including elderly users and those with disabilities.

DESIGN FOR ALL

The philosophy of Design for All is best summarised as "The design of products, services and environments to be usable by all people, to the greatest extent possible, without the need for adaptation or specialised design". This does not mean that designers are expected to design every product to be usable by every consumer as this would be an impracticable, if not impossible, target. It has to be acknowledged that there will always be some people who, because of their severe impairments, need specialist equipment or assistive technology to modify the method of making input to, or receiving output from, some piece of mainstream technology.

It must be remembered that Design for All is not just a process of adding an extra feature to a product to meet the perceived needs of a disabled user. It is a process, like quality, which has to be considered at every stage in developing a new product or service. This requires companies to promote a culture of inclusion within their organisation. It also requires detailed technical guidelines on the design features required by the various groups of disabled users.

Adopting "Design for All" when designing ICT products and services can be illustrated by a three level model:

1. Mainstream products designed according to good Human Factors practice, incorporating considerations for people with impairments, which can be used by a broad range of users;

2. Products that are adaptable to permit the connection of assistive technology devices;

3. Specially designed or tailored products for very disabled users.

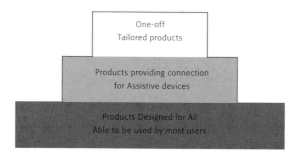

As long as "Design for All" is adopted from the start of the design process, it is possible to design products accessible to a significant number of disabled and elderly people with minimum effort and cost. Designing more usable mainstream products based on the "Design for All" philosophy is not only of benefit to the end user - it can also offer benefits to business. Considering the needs of older and mentally disabled people can help create simple and error-friendly products, which can reach a much broader market of people who at the moment could be described as "technologically abstinent".

Designing mainstream products for users with special requirements can also often bring benefits to other users and thus increase a product's marketability. Most users may benefit from the increased usability that "Design for All" brings. For example, control of volume amplification in telephones was originally developed for people with hearing problems but it is has also been found useful for anyone using a telephone in a noisy environment such as a dealing room, train station or factory. Thus a telecommunications design that kept the needs of the greatest number of people in mind (including people who are hard of hearing) provided an attractive feature for all users. Furthermore, when volume amplification is built into the original design of a telephone, the cost is inconsequential.

Taking account of the needs of people with visual impairment can also help those users trying to read a display in poor lighting conditions or without their reading glasses to hand. A product designed to be easily used by those with restricted movement or strength can also help those struggling with children or luggage. It is important to remember that there is no clear boundary between people who are categorised as "disabled" and those who are not. Performance, or ability distribution, for a given skill or ability is generally a continuous function. For example, for every person who has severe visual problems there are numerous others who wear glasses or who could benefit from a larger label on a product that is easier to see in the poor light. In addition there are many people who pass though periods of temporary disability due to some injury.

It should also be noted that in order to maintain and develop sales in the US market, all European companies need to be aware of the growing amount of legislation in this field. For example, under regulations which took effect in the US in June 2001 issued under Section 508 of the Rehabilitation Act of 1973, all technology purchased by federal agencies in the US must be accessible to disabled users, with few exceptions.

This is having the effect that large American corporations are already incorporating accessibility, or "Design for All", into products that they also sell into Europe. This is because they do not wish to develop separate products for the European market and they also see the demand for accessible products expanding to state governments and schools. European companies wishing to maintain/develop their US market also need to adopt a "Design for All" approach for their products.

Any prudent company should assume that similar legislative trends are following within Europe.

USERS

In Human Factors terms, "user" refers to any person who uses, maintains or is affected by the use of the system under consideration. An understanding of the intended user must be at the core of the overall design process. A proper analysis of the user requirements is essential and should always be included in the initial requirements specification. With a computer or a cashpoint terminal there is only one user at a time, whereas in a normal telephone call, there are usually two users, the initiator of the call and the receiver of the call.

It is instructive to note that the group of users that is all too often the apparent model for equipment and service designers is likely to be male, late 20's to late 40's, engineers or at least university graduates, and familiar with technology and its potential benefits. In order to have achieved this status, it is likely that they will have average hearing, sight and manual dexterity, as all education systems unfortunately tend to select in these areas by default. They will, however, have a 7% (i.e. 1 in 14) chance of being red/green colour blind.

Reliance on this model, however, can be seen on second thoughts to be quite obviously defective. It fails to recognise the differences within the business community resulting from those social changes that have increased the number of female members of this group over recent years. It fails also to recognise the movement of labour within the European Union, and the changes that occur with age. Furthermore, since age changes begin to take effect even from the mid 40's, assumptions of ability at age 30 may not apply so readily at 48.

Within the Design for All process, the designer must consider the likely user populations and their characteristics. A PC might be aimed at the whole population, whereas a game system might be aimed primarily at younger users. Regarding the intended users, it is necessary to consider the spread of their characteristics and their individual differences. Within this process, the designer should aim to ensure that all user requirements are addressed and should give positive support towards integrating the requirements of children, the elderly and other people with special needs.

There are a large number of attributes that can be used to distinguish between people in a population and in this area it is useful to refer to the classification of human abilities and the consequences of impairment given in ISO/IEC Guide 71 [1]. The ones that should be considered to have direct impact on the successful use of ICT products and services include:

- *Sensory abilities* such as seeing, hearing, touch, taste, smell and balance.
- *Physical abilities* such as speech, dexterity, manipulation, mobility and strength.
- *Cognitive abilities* such as intellect, memory, language and literacy.

Allergies can also be a significant factor for some products.

In this Guide, each of the specified abilities and disabilities is identified and described in sufficient detail to give an introduction to the understanding of the resultant handicaps.

Aging will cause a change or degradation of many user characteristics. In general, most functional abilities will change with age. For example, older people tend to lose their ability to detect higher frequency sounds (see figure 1) and many use a hearing aid.

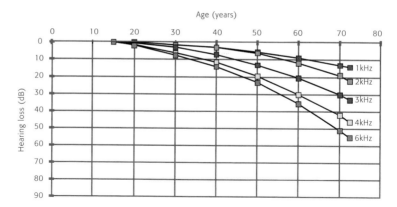

Figure 1 Hearing level as a function of age for non-noise exposed subjects (after Glorig [2]).

The incidence and severity of visual impairment increases with age and the changes in the physical structure of the eye will lead, among other effects, to loss of visual acuity (the ability to see fine detail), the inability to accommodate changes of focus between short and long distances and a loss of speed of adaptation to changing light levels. Manual dexterity, mobility, strength and endurance also decline with age. These effects are often accompanied by a slowing of the brain's ability to process information, causing difficulty in taking in, attending to and discriminating between sensory information. This has the effect of causing an overall slow-ing of "behaviour" and the phenomenon, generally described as a "loss of memory", which is sometimes referred to as "a senior moment".

Recognising the variation in ability across a sample of popu-lation, there is clearly a point at which ability becomes so far from the expected range for the population that it has to be considered outside (above or below) the expected range. Dis-ability, by its definition, occurs where some ability falls below the expected range. Population figures are, however, very difficult to collect because of differences between the vari-ous national views of the onset of disability and the differing methods of collecting national statistics. In some countries, for example, soldiers wounded in action are not counted as 'disabled', for reasons such as pension schemes, even though their physical or cognitive impairments make them just as disabled as those who are registered as such.

Even the Statistical Office of the European Communities (Eurostat) states, in its disabled persons statistical data [3], "in spite of the large number of disabled persons, there are still no reliable European-level statistics in this field". This publication gives access to the information that exists, but it is limited in the countries covered and the information provided. Clearly much of the existing and often quoted published data must have been derived by extrapolation.

In 2001 Eurostat published the results of a survey on disability [4] in 14 European countries (the EU 15 minus Sweden for which no data was available). This survey showed that, of the population aged from 16 to 64, 4.5% reported that they suffered from severe disability and another 10% suffered moderate disability. Unfortunately, this survey did not include those under 16, and more importantly, those over 64.

Figure 2, taken from the same survey, shows how the percentage of people reporting disability in any age group increases with age. It can therefore be expected that the population aged 65 and over would report a significantly increased percentage of disability. Reference [3] suggests that in the over 80 age group some 50% to 60% are disabled.

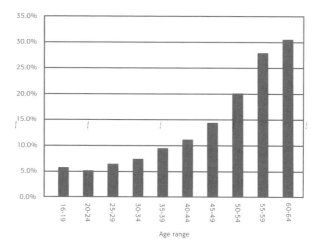

Figure 2: Age-specific percentages of persons reporting disability

Thus, assuming some 20% of the population to be over 65 [5] and taking as a minimum that an average of 33% of these are disabled, this would suggest that approximately at least an additional 6% of the population are disabled and elderly, giving a total of about 20% of the population with moderate or severe disability.

This figure indicates the potential size of this market as a proportion of the entire market for ICT products and services.

THE HUMAN-CENTRED DESIGN PROCESS

One important reason to adopt a Human-Centred Design approach to ICT equipment is the legal regulation on the minimum safety and health requirements for work with display screen equipment. (EU Directive 90/270 [6]), which among its articles requires the employer "to perform an analysis of workstations in order to evaluate the safety and health conditions to which they give rise for their workers, particularly as regards the possible risks to eyesight, physical problems and problems of mental stress". It also requires that "consultation and participation of workers----shall take place----on the matters covered by this Directive". These are a set of very human centred requirements.

According to ISO 13407 [7], the incorporation of a human-centred approach is characterised by:

a) the active involvement of users and clear understanding of]user and task requirements;

b) an appropriate allocation of functions between users and technology;

c) the iteration of design solutions;

d) multidisciplinary design.

The users and developers should interact throughout the design process. The nature of user involvement varies depending on the design activities that are being undertaken, noting that the type of product has an effect. When designing a one-off product for a particular user, the actual user can be directly linked to the design process. When designing quantity produced consumer products, appropriate representatives of the planned user groups should be involved in the design process.

The aim of the technology is to assist the user to carry out selected tasks. The design process should identify all the tasks to be carried out and define which parts of the tasks are taken care of by technology and which parts are the user's responsibilities. Decisions cannot just be based on letting the technology do what it is capable of doing and allocating the remaining functions to the user. The human functions should form a meaningful set of tasks.

In iterative design, feedback from the users is a critical source of information. The exact user requirements cannot be defined at the beginning of a design process. On the one hand, the designers may not have a clear idea of what the users might want. On the other hand, the users may not have a clear idea what the technology could make possible. The current context of use is only the starting point of the design. The planned new system may change the context of use and then again the new context of use may change the user requirements for the technology. The design process should support this iteration by visualising the design decisions and evaluating them with the users in the planned context of use. As the result of the evaluation, both the context of use and the design may be refined.

Human-Centred Design requires a variety of skills. Depending on the nature of the system to be developed, the multi-disciplinary team may include end-users, management, application field experts, system designers, marketing experts, visual designers, human factors experts, and trainers. An individual team member may represent different skill areas and viewpoints. The minimum team consists of the designer and the user.

GUIDELINES

A useful source of guidance on Design for All can be found in the ETSI guide EG 202 116 [8] This document describes means of evaluating the designs using either an analytical checklist approach or by usability testing, and details are given of both of these methods. An Annex to the Guide provides details of checklists and suggests methods of presenting the results.

The document then moves on to provide a set of detailed guidelines, which for ease of use are logically grouped and all treated in a consistent form with definition, cross references, recommendations and sometimes comments. It commences with general design issues such as adaptability, colour, consistency, error management, feedback, flexibility and response times and then covers dialogue styles, assistive technology, multimedia presentation, labels, national variations, security and user support.

The next section gives specific guidelines dealing with input components starting with tactile inputs such as keyboards, pointing devices, switches, variable controls and software controls. Guidance on acoustic inputs covers microphones and speech recognition and visual input deals with cameras, head and eye movement and scanners. Iris recognition and fingerprints are the only biometric inputs dealt with as they are considered the most advanced. The section covering electronic input deals with card readers, machine readable cards, contactless cards and Bar code readers.

The section on output components treats visual outputs such as visual displays of various types, their characteristics and quality requirements, and also visual indicators such as simple optical signals and icons. Acoustic outputs deal with non-speech audio such as tones, earcons, ring signals and music. Speech output and auditory menus also come in this section. Final clauses cover tactile outputs such as markers and Braille, vibrotactile indication and force feedback together with a short treatment of printed output.

The final parts of the guide give additional product-specific guidelines for items such as cords, casework, connectors, handsets, portable equipment and videophones. Service specific guidelines cover such matters as addresses, call handling, transmission, dialling, phone based interfaces, supplementary services and voice transmission.

Wherever possible, the design recommendations give objective data specifying the requirements of given features. The whole guide is fully indexed to assist the user to find his way around what is a fairly large document of some 200 pages.

ASSISTIVE TECHNOLOGY

It is clear that design for all cannot totally satisfy the needs of all disabled users. Such an aim would be impractical, if not totally impossible. Design for All must in practice remain "Design for Most" [9]. There will always remain some people who, because of their severe impairments, are unable to operate well-designed mainstream ICT products and services because there still remains a gap between their capabilities and the requirements of the user interface. To enable disabled and elderly people to lead full and independent lives thus requires two complementary approaches, the Design for All approach and the Assistive Technology (AT) approach. Even then there will remain a few users who cannot physically manage to operate some equipment, even using some assistive device.

This situation can be illustrated by the well known usability triangle where the broad base represents the bulk of users who can access most services without help, rising to those who need some sort of adaptation such as enlarged font, then up to a smaller number who need assistive technology to use a service, leaving a very small number at the peak of the triangle who cannot manage without the assistance of a carer.

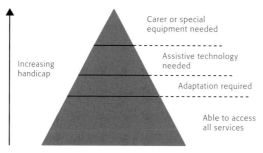

The usability triangle

Design for All can move upwards the boundary between those able to access all services and those who require adaptation. It can even move up the lower boundary of those who require assistive technology to access a service.

Unfortunately neither Design for All nor assistive technology can assist those few at the peak of the triangle and in these cases a one off specially built piece of equipment or the assistance of a carer will be needed.

To enable an assistive device to be used in conjunction with other ICT equipment, the ICT equipment must be provided with some interface to which the external assistive device can be connected. This interface should be made to an open standard. A well known example of this in practice is the way in which a special ergonomic keyboard can readily replace a standard keyboard on a PC. The provision of such a standard interface is an aspect of design for all that is often overlooked.

The ICT equipment should be designed in such a way that:

a) A person who is operating the device via assistive technology can use all of its relevant functions.

b) It can be easily and simply connected to the assistive technology device.

c) It has a standard method of interfacing with the assistive technology device and uses standard control commands.

d) It is designed to maximise the number of people who can operate it with standard assistive technology devices.

It is reasonable to assume that no assistive device should demand special additional power from the device with which it is working. If it requires power additional to that normally available at the interface, it should provide this itself.

General guidance on the use of assistive technology with ICT equipment may be found in ETSI Technical Report TR 102 068 [10] which aims to set out the needs of users of assistive technology and to give guidance on the connection of assistive devices to mainstream ICT equipment. This report notes that the user needs can be viewed in two different ways. One is from an expert's technical view of satisfying the particular demands arising from a given disability. The other might be termed a "wish list" as expressed by users. The first can be satisfied by a paper study. The second requires posing questions to users.

From a technical point of view, a person with any disability will require assistive technology to use a particular item of ICT equipment whenever they:

- Cannot operate the controls (for instance because of their physical disability)

- Cannot obtain information from the device (for instance because of their sensory disability)

- Cannot understand how to operate the device (for in stance if they have a cognitive disability)

There may also be occasions where the operation of the device would be possible but would cause the user pain or take too much effort. These are the physical needs that require to be satisfied. The Technical report [10] sets out these user needs in a similar form to that in the design for all guide [8] and some examples are given of useful assistive technologies.

During the preparation of TR 102 068 [10], two question-naires were sent out to try to determine what disabled users actually felt they needed. The first was sent to a number of professionals working in the disability field and the second to a representative sample of the manufacturers and designers of assistive technology devices with the aim of finding out if there was any consensus as to which of the disabled users would require assistive technology and which technology they would use it with. With the time and staff available it was not found possible to question many individual disabled users.

There was a good response to the first questionnaire but unfortunately there were some differing interpretations of the intent of the question structure, which made it difficult to analyse the results. The questions in the second question-naire were open ended and so the replies once again did not lead themselves to simple analysis.

In spite of the difficulties in close analysis of the two questionnaires it was felt that the replies contained a significant amount of useful information in the field of disability which it was worth making public for other workers in the field, if only as an instructive warning on the need to run a trial before embarking on any survey. They were therefore recorded in a second ETSI technical report TR 102 279 "Two surveys on assistive technology" [11].

In the first questionnaire the majority of respondents felt that design for all was important and should cover many disabilities. Many respondents pointed up the value of speech recognition and text to speech translation facilities. Cost was one of the problems repeatedly identified by many respondents although weight and portability were felt important for assistive devices. Most responses identified particular features that were desired on various types of ICT equipment and a general need was expressed for real access to the coming world of electronic information and commerce.

The majority of manufacturers who responded wanted standard interfaces for the connection of assistive devices. There was a majority opinion that the protocols should be independent of the transmission system, although some expressed the caveat that where an interconnection technology had its own standards they should be followed. Many said that there should be two-way communication between the ICT device and the AT device. A wish was expressed that any such standard should not stifle future innovation. Some suggested that creating awareness of a standard was an important factor.

The first report [10] lists the input and output requirements of the user interface of ICT devices that need to be replaced by assistive devices at the man-machine interface. These are characterised and the assistive devices are listed and classified. This classification follows that of ISO 9999 [12], which covers a vast number of devices ranging from abacuses and abdominal hernia aids to zip pullers and zippers, but as only a few of the devices listed in that standard have the potential to be interconnected to information and communication technology (ICT) systems they are identified as examples.

The listing notes that in some cases the assistive device may be a mainstream item such as a cordless or mobile telephone, which can become a really liberating tool for a wheelchair bound user.

TECHNICAL SOLUTIONS

When preparing the report [10], close liaison was maintained with industry to try to ensure ready acceptance of the result-ant recommendations and to bring about a consensus among key manufacturers in order to obtain a sound basis for the specification of these interfaces. These liaisons revealed just what was feasible within the requirements of the telecommu-nications industry and unfortunately it was not found pos-sible to standardise on one single interface, whether wired or wireless.

The signals crossing the assistive device interface can be broadly classified into those control and status signals neces-sary to the ICT device and into communications signals. Control signals would include the mouse/pointer output, a translated speech command from a voice operated assistive device and number information in a communications device. Status signals from any device could indicate its readiness to operate or accept signal input. Communication signals can be assumed to be the fundamental information intended to be input to and output from the device, such as speech, text or video information.

Assisive device/service	Data			Audio	Video
	Control and status	Text	Graphics		
Braille display	⬅➡	➡			
Tactual graphics display	⬅➡	➡	➡		
Synthetic speech display	⬅➡	➡			
Enhanced visual display	⬅➡	➡	➡		
Keyboard/pointer	⬅➡	⬅	⬅		
Speech recognition	⬅➡	⬅			
Hearing aid	⬅➡			➡	
Tactile aid	⬅➡			➡	
Alarm/monitor system	⬅➡			➡	➡
Smart house	⬅➡	⬅➡	⬅➡	⬅➡	⬅➡
Navigation system	⬅➡	⬅➡	➡	➡	➡

NOTE 1:   ➡ indicates information to assistive device;
  ⬅ indicates information from assistive device;
  ⬅➡ indicates information in both directions.

NOTE 2:   Some systems may use fewer modes than the possible ones indicated.

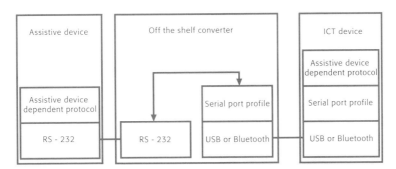

Examples of information exchanged with assistive device

237

The table shows some examples of the type of information that might be exchanged between various items of ICT equipment and assistive devices.

The simplest possible interfaces should always be used. These can be used with a number of wired or wireless transmission technologies, supporting these basic connections.

TR 102 068 [10] reviews both the wired and wireless transmission technologies that may be used at the interface between an ICT device and an assistive device and simple descriptions are given of their differing main features. A brief introduction to protocol stacks is provided for those new to the subject and a number of useful existing standard protocols are noted.

In order to encourage harmonisation, recommendations are made of the preferred interface and protocols to be used for various types of connection. USB is the currently preferred solution for the wired interface, HiperLAN2 or the IEEE 802.11 family for wireless local area networking and Bluetooth (IEE 802.15) for wireless personal area networking and access. It was considered at the time that DECT was not likely to achieve wide use due to limitations in its global availability.

RS-232 interface transmission over USB or Bluetooth

a) The RS-232 interface is recommended for data. The report gives illustrations of connections using various interfaces and protocols showing how standard systems can be used. The example shows how RS-232 interface transmission can be arranged over a USB or Bluetooth connection using an off the shelf converter.

In the telecommunications industry, the AT command set has become the standard protocol for the transfer of control and status information. It is commonly used to test mobile telephones during their production. The AT command set is defined in ITU-T V.250 [13] and in ETSI TS 100 916 [14]. Unfortunately the information in the TS is not readily comprehensible except by a mobile telephone expert.

The report [10] originally proposed a special AT command to be used to identify any command string originating from an assistive device but this suggestion was found not to be acceptable to the worldwide mobile telephone industry as it was thought that it would lead to non-standard solutions.

It was recommended that the audio interface should be similar to that used in Personal Computers but no recommendations could be made for video due to the rapid development in this area.

Recently further research has been conducted within the Human Factors Group on the AT command set suitable for use with assistive devices and a document has been written (TS 102 511) [15] which associates the standard AT commands with the requirements of assistive devices and identifies some new commands that could be necessary. This TS attempted to make more approachable the technicalities of the command software set out in the AT command set standard [14], mainly by describing some usage scenarios. Whilst the usage scenarios may be of interest, the software requirements are still highly complex.

TS 102 511 [15] identifies some new commands that could be necessary for certain useful assistive functions but this aspect of the work is not yet fully complete as further cooperation will be necessary with the mobile telephone industry to standardise these commands within the mobile environment.

THE DEMONSTRATOR

Arising from the original work on the technical report, a demonstrator model was produced of an assistive device (a Braille personal assistant) capable of interworking with a range of mobile telephones. The personal assistant provided the normal personal assistant functions of a diary, telephone directory etc. but with a Braille input keyboard and a text to speech translator providing the output.

When coupled to a mobile telephone through a wired connection using a simple RS 232 interface, the dialling of numbers was supported as well as full text messaging facilities.

This model provided a working example of an effective assistive device and showed how different makes of mobile phones could be controlled by an external device over a simple interface.

CONCLUSIONS

For assistive devices to become affordable and effective, the significant players in each field need to agree on a set of protocols to be used in the communication between assistive devices and the relevant ICT devices. As the report [10] identifies, in general it is not necessary to develop either new protocols or new hardware interfaces. The interface and protocol standards should be chosen from those already available so as to form a coherent set which covers all major aspects of information exchange between the two sets of devices.

In spite of the work on TS 102 511 [15], achieving this will still require the upgrading of existing standards where the necessary commands do not exist, or the writing of new standards where no existing standard is relevant. Consensus on this set of interface standards must be reached in the appropriate standards forums in a process which involves manufacturers of mainstream devices, manufacturers of assistive devices and groups representing users with different special needs.

REFERENCES

[1] ISO/IEC Guide 71 (2001): "Guidelines for standards developers to address the needs of older persons and persons with disability".

[2] Glorig, Ward, Nixon: "Damage risk criteria and noise induced hearing loss". NPL conference on Control of Noise, 1961.

[3] "Disabled persons statistical data" 2nd Ed. European Commission 1995.

[4] "Disability and social participation in Europe" Eurostat 2001.

[5] Roe, Patrick R. W. (ed.) (2001). "Bridging the GAP? Access to telecommunications for all people." - The Commission of the European Communities.

[6] "Directive 90/270/EEC on the minimum safety and health requirements for work with display screen equipment" OJ L 156, 21/06/1990 pp 14-18.

[7] ISO/IEC 13407: Human-centred design processes for interactive systems".

[8] ETSI EG 202 116: "Human Factors; Guidelines for ICT

products and services; "Design for All""

[9] W J Mellors, "Design for all guidelines for ICT products and services", in Proc. 18th International Symposium on Human Factors in Telecommunications, Bergen 2001 pp. 285-288.

[10] ETSI TR 102 068, "Human Factors; Requirements for assistive technology devices in ICT".

[11] ETSI TR 102 279, "Human Factors; Two surveys on assistive technology".

[12] ISO 9999: "Technical aids for disabled persons – Classification".

[13] ITU-T V250 (05/99): "Serial asynchronous automatic dialling and control".

[14] ETSI TS 100 916: "Digital cellular telecommunications system (Phase 2+); AT commands set for GSM Mobile Equipment (ME)".

[15] ETSI TS 102 511, "AT Commands for Assistive Mobile Device Interfaces ".

KRISTIN SKEIDE FUGLERUD is Cand. Scient (MSc.) in information systems from the University of Oslo, Norway. She is a senior research scientist at Norwegian Computing Center, which is a non profit research institute in Oslo. Here she has worked for the last seven years. Her primary research interests are universal design, e-accessibility, human computer interaction and user centred systems development. She also has about 10 years of experience of the Norwegian ICT industry as a consultant. Here she worked with programming and systems development. She has also provided training and supervision for different types of personnel in the use of various software packages.

UNIVERSAL DESIGN IN ICT SERVICES

Kristin Skeide Fuglerud

ICT IS EVERYWHERE

Many activities in our societies, ranging from leisure to work and participation in various social units, structures and organisations are increasingly dependent on information and communication technology (ICT [1]). Also many services in important areas such as government, education, health, culture, travel, commerce and others are increasingly migrating to the digital environment. Because ICT is everywhere, being able to access and use ICT has become a prerequisite to be able to take part fully in society.

Universal Design is a design strategy to make products and services accessible and usable to as many people as possible. This chapter presents arguments for Universal Design in ICT services and discusses the importance of integrating Universal Design activities into the development process of such services.

ICT PRODUCTS AND ICT SERVICES

There is no clear-cut line between ICT products and ICT services. ICT services are usually delivered through a network and you may access a service through ICT products, such as devices (e.g. PC, mobile, digital TV) and software (e.g. web browser, e-mail). An ICT service involves a service provider each time it is used, whereas a product is separable from a certain service provider. In general an ICT service is accessed and used by many more users at the same time than a product is.

ICT services vary greatly in complexity, from simple informational services, such as web pages, to what we can call transactional services. Transactional services are integrated with the service providers' business processes (e.g. e-business with order-systems), and sometimes with services from other service providers (e.g. payment services). Services often have both internal users (working for the service provider) and external users (other service providers and customers). The tasks of the internal users are usually quite different from those of the external users. Often the internal and the external users communicate indirectly through the service. The internal users may edit information for the external users, or handle requests from external users.

Especially when developing complex ICT services there will be many stakeholders and many considerations to take into account. In order to succeed with Universal Design in such situations, it is necessary to ensure that it is high on the agenda, and to get the mandate and resources to undertake necessary activities. The designer will often have to educate the different stakeholders, especially the service owner and the management, about Universal Design. Then, as early as possible, one should consider how to integrate Universal Design activities into the overall project life cycle and software development process.

UNIVERSAL DESIGN IN ICT AND RELATED CONCEPTS

The integration of all users into the information society, often referred to as e-inclusion, has become an important policy goal internationally. To achieve this it is essential to design mainstream products and services accessible to as broad a range of users as possible, including older people, people with disabilities and also people in changing or constraining environments.

Several design approaches that encompass the goal of producing more inclusive products and services have emerged within ICT development communities since the mid-1980's. Examples of these are "universal design", "design for all", "universal usability", "accessible design", "universal access", and "sensitive inclusive design".

There are some differences between the approaches, but the similarities and the goal of design for diversity are more important. There is a large potential for creating better and more usable products by adopting the main idea, being aware of the reasons for doing so.

WHY SHOULD WE CARE ABOUT UNIVERSAL DESIGN IN ICT?

Benefits for the individual and for society
Many activities in our society depend on access to and ability to use ICT tools and services. We use ICT for finding information, to access public services, in education, to find and qualify for work, as a means for social communication, or for electronic commerce.

The Internet is one of our most important channels for communication and information, which in turn is vital to participation in social and democratic activities. When family members live far apart from each other, being able to communicate electronically, exchange pictures, videos, have video conversations with web cameras etc. can make it easier to maintain contact. Many social organisations communicate with their members mainly through digital channels. People with low ICT competence may find it increasingly difficult to find a job. Statistics shows that people with low literacy and low computer knowledge also suffer wage loss compared to skilled counterparts (Statistics Canada and OECD et al. 2005).

---

1 The term ICT - Information and Communications Technology (or Technologies) covers all forms of computer and communications equipment and software used to create, store, transmit, interpret, and manipulate information in various digital formats (e.g. text, business data, voice conversations, still images, audio, film and multimedia). It is used about any combination of information technology, telecommunications and data networking technologies.

In the western world there is a trend towards e-government, which is use of ICT to exchange information with and offer services to citizens and businesses. The most important anticipated benefits of e-government include improved efficiency, convenience, and better accessibility of public services. Efficiency of these services depends on widespread uptake and use in the population.

It is not only public services that are digitised. Our entire society is transformed into a self-service society, where citizens, customers and consumers help themselves by using electronic services. Examples of such services are paying bills through the Internet bank, filling out and sending the tax return electronically, finding and buying tickets for travel or events from either ticket machines or through the Internet, e-learning, filling out and sending electronic forms etc. Being able to use these ICT services means that people become more flexible and independent as to where and when to do each task, and sometimes it also means cheaper services.

At the same time the western world is faced with huge challenges because the population is growing older. As the population ages, accessibility challenges and disabling conditions will escalate, increasing the need for society to find ways to accommodate people with disabilities and age-related impairments. This is also the case in working life. Changes in vision, hearing and manual dexterity affect people's ability to use ICTs (Mosner, Spiezle & Emerman 2003).

In addition to growing economic and social considerations, the issue of e-inclusion has become a question of human rights and democracy. As a consequence many states are extending their laws in order to strengthen rights to equal access to information, products and services.

BENEFITS FOR THE SERVICE PROVIDER

There are many reasons for service providers to aim at Universal Design. If they are selling solutions to the public market they have to consider these issues because of public procurement policies and legislations. Two European Directives on Public Procurement (2004/17/EC and 2004/18/EC) direct public bodies to ensure that design for all principles are taken into account in the technical specifications of all products and services which are procured using public finances. However, legislation is far from the only reason why service providers should aim at Universal Design.

Universal Design means thorough consideration of users and their tasks. This will increase their potential customer base, without increasing the need for customer service personnel. When the user interface is usable and accessible it is easier to distribute registration work to the customer, reducing the need for double registration (for example that a customer fills in a paper form which is then interpreted and registered by a customer service representative). It also may increase information quality. When the customer enters his/her own information, errors made because of misinterpretation by the customer service will be eliminated.

Universal Design means following standards that make the service operable with diverse types of technology such as assistive technology (both devices and software). For example the service should work with browsers from different vendors (such as Internet Explorer, Mozilla, Opera etc.). This will increase the customer base because people can use it with their preferred technology. Another advantage is that the service will be less dependent on the customers' current version of software and the types of device they are using. It makes it easier to deal with the pace of technology change and variety of equipment that users employ (Shneiderman 2000).

There is a trend towards more mobile devices and services. In many European countries, the prevalence of mobile phones is rapidly approaching the prevalence level of TV. The mobile phone is becoming common property. In fact, the number of mobile phone connections is increasing all over the world (ITU 2007). This development introduces new challenges to the design of ICT services. Making a service operable with different types of devices (e.g. PCs, PDAs, mobiles and digital TV), and especially mobile equipment, makes it accessible in more types of situations which again may increase the sales of the service.

Designing for diversity encourages modularity and partitioning of the software. A simple example of this is the use of Cascading Style Sheets (CSS) which makes it possible to separate the content of websites from the presentation of it. This makes it easier to maintain the solution while adapting to new requirements, such as a new web browser or screen readers[2].

The possibilities for making universally designed ICT have never been better. It is only our lack of imagination and creativity that constrains us. The material costs are usually low compared with other areas such as buildings and environments. In many cases ideas and software could be reused. Technology and functionality used in GPS based navigations systems in cars could for example be reused in technology to help blind people find their way. Eye tracking technology makes people who are not able to move, speak or even use their facial muscles able to communicate. People with sign language as their mother tongue (born deaf) can use mobile phones with video conferencing functionality to have a distance conversation in sign language etc.

Many service owners and developers are afraid of the costs of Universal Design. They have the misconception that it is necessary to develop new features from the ground up for small and special user groups. But, it is not a question of developing new assistive technology, it is rather a question of following guidelines and standards that make it possible to use assistive technology in conjunction with the service. Guidelines

---

[2] A screen reader is an assistive technology often used by blind and visually impaired people. It interprets what is being displayed on a screen, and the content can be presented either as synthetic speech or via a Braille strips.

and standards can usually be implemented at little cost (NCD 2001). In addition there are many technologies already developed that could be adjusted, integrated or serve as inspiration for Universal Design of ICT services. Multimodal interaction is an example of this.

MULTIMODAL INTERACTION

It is possible to interact with ICTs through different modes. Depending upon the device, users could be able to provide input via keystrokes, mouse, speech, and handwriting. Output could be presented via displays, pre-recorded or synthetic speech, audio, and tactile mechanisms such as mobile phone vibrators and Braille displays. Multimodality refers to support for transformations to alternative modes, such that more than one modality is available to interact with the services.

Information in electronic format constitutes an ideal basis for Universal Design, because it can be transformed in all these different ways. Obrenovic, Abascal & Starcevic (2007) point out that there is a fundamental connection between multimodal interface design and universal accessibility. A person with low hearing is depending on visual or haptic alarms instead of audio (e.g. beeps). A blind person or a person using his eyes for other tasks would prefer information presented in another modality than visual, such as audio or haptic (e.g. Braille). It is also advisable to utilize several types of media and modalities to facilitate comprehension for people with cognitive disabilities. For example, a functionality that reads a sentence out loud while the user follows the text on a screen may be very useful for many people with reading disabilities. See more examples from the W3C device independence working group (W3C 2005a).

Being able to utilize different modalities is also necessary when designing for changing contexts and situations, and thus supporting mobility. For example if there is much noise (e.g. a production room) or when silence is preferred (e.g. a meeting), a system notification in visual or haptic form (e.g. vibrating mobile phones) might be more suitable than an audio alarm.

CONSTRAINTS IN THE USE CONTEXT OF ICTS

Often conditions or constraints in the context of use of ICT products or services, such as an activity or situation, produce similar requirements of an ICT-service to a specific impairment. Such conditions can be referred to as an "impairing environment". For example, an ICT-service used in a situation where the user's eyes are busy with other things (e.g. driving) must be operable without vision. For blind users the ICT-service should also be operable without vision. Similarly, an ICT service for use in a very silent environment (such as a meeting) should be operable without sound/audio. An ICT-service for use by a hearing impaired person should also be operable without audio.

The following table shows how constraints in the environment may produce similar requirements of an ICT service to those called for by impairments. The list is not necessarily exhaustive, but illustrates the point. The examples in the table are adapted from Vanderheiden (2000).

CONSTRAINING SITUA-TION OR CONTEXT	CORRESPONDING IMPAIRMENT	REQUIRES OF AN ICT SERVICE	EXAMPLES OF ALTERNA-TIVE DESIGN SOLU-TIONS
People in situation where the eyes are very busy such as driving a car or when complete darkness is necessary.	People who are blind	Operable without vision	Present information with haptic feedback sound or speech, and/or provide compatibility with assistive technology such as screen readers (Braille or text to speech functionality).
People using a small display or in a smoky environment, with difficult light conditions such as sun reflections or sunset.	People who are visually impaired	Operable with low vision	Present information with haptic feedback sound or speech, and/or provide compatibility with assistive technology such as screen readers (Braille or text to speech functionality).

CONSTRAINING SITUA-TION OR CONTEXT	CORRESPONDING IMPAIRMENT	REQUIRES OF AN ICT SERVICE	EXAMPLES OF ALTERNA-TIVE DESIGN SOLU-TIONS
People in a very noisy environment (music, traffic, ma-chines) or in forced silence (library or meeting).	People that are deaf	Operable with no hearing	Present informa-tion with visual or haptic feedback and/or provide compatibility for assistive technol-ogy for deaf people such as speech to text or speech to sign language.
Noisy environments or when ears are busy	People who are hear-ing impaired	Operable with limited hearing	Present information with visual or haptic feedback and/or pro-vide for compatibility for deaf people.
People who need to wear gloves because they are outdoors in cold weather, or because they are workers on a construction site, or need to wear a chemical suit, or who are in a bouncing vehicle.	People with a phys-ical disability, such as having muscu-loskeletal disorders, being lame, lacking limbs etc.	Operable with limited manual dexterity	Make objects to be manipulated large, allow for speech input and/or provide for compatibility with assistive de-vices such as special keyboards, joysticks, eye tracking devices.
People who are distracted, stressed or panicked or under the influence of drugs	People with a cognitive disability, such as difficulties in remembering,	Operable with limited cognition	Clear and concise formulations. No excess information. Limit number of choices.
People who haven't learned to read a language, people who are visitors, people who left reading glasses behind, or visually impaired people without access to assistive technol-ogy such as screen readers.	people with a reading disability or visually impaired	Operable without reading	Possibility of select-ing language, using audio output such as speech (synthetic or recorded), and illustrative icons, drawings, pictures or videos.
People who have a device with limited input methods (a mobile device), and people wearing gloves (outdoors in cold weather, or workers on a construction site), a chemical suit or who are in a bouncing vehicle.	People with a writing disability (dyslectic) people who have problems in spelling in this language. People who have limited manual dexterity.	Operable without writing	Let user select between predefined alternatives, use speech recognition.

Table 1 Situations, impairments and requirements

INCORPORATING A UNIVERSAL DESIGN APPROACH INTO THE DESIGN PROCESS

The development of electronic services is usually carried out by teams in a software development organisation, often following a process model. There are several popular models for developing and designing software, and most of them are based on iterative development and customer/user involvement, but they have little or no guidance on designing for diversity in users and use situations. The selection of a process model depends on a number of factors such as the culture of the development organisation, quality procedures, the customer, budgets and schedules, the market, the type of service and so on. Rather than advising a new model for Universal Design, it will often be better to integrate activities promoting Universal Design throughout the actual development process or project life cycle.

An iterative and user centred development process is a good basis for Universal Design. It is especially important that the methodology used is able to handle changing requirements as result of user feedback, usability testing, and the need for interoperability with other devices and technologies (Perlman 2002). Some issues that should be attended to in connection with the development process are discussed below.

KNOWLEDGE, ATTITUDE AND COMMITMENT IN THE DEVELOPMENT ORGANISATION

Universal Design is very much about the knowledge, motivation and attitudes of the design team. It is important to make sure that the team members understand what Universal Design is, and why they should follow this approach in their project. Much can be achieved if the design team is determined and focused on diversity in users and use contexts from the beginning. However the best results are likely to be achieved when you have commitment and support from the service or project owner and the management. Universal Design should be made an explicit and high level goal, which is often necessary in order to get resources for Universal Design activities and priorities within the project. However, commitment from team members and team leaders is also important. A research study was conducted in the US to find what changes in law or practice would have most impact on achieving accessibility of ICT products and services (NCD 2001). This study concluded that personal commitment and individual leadership were the most important factors for success (NCD 2001).

Therefore it is important to make sure that there is some-one within the design team who has the responsibility for keeping a Universal Design focus throughout the project. In small projects, this could be the designer or project leader. In larger projects, you might need a person specially dedicated to Universal Design issues. It is essential that this person has the mandate and authority to influence the development process and priorities.

It is wise to start with a description of the ICT service and its main objectives. For a public transport company this might be to make it easy for travellers to plan their trip, to get more people to use public transport and to reduce the need for personal service for travellers. For an insurance company one goal might be to let the customer select and combine insurance products for their own needs on their own. The overall user population should be described, and Universal Design should, as mentioned above, be included as an overall objective for the service. It is often useful to describe some use scenarios, i.e. using short stories or narratives of use situations, which can be extended and elaborated during the development process.

ITERATIONS, USER INVOLVEMENT AND CHANGING REQUIREMENTS

As pointed out in the introduction to this section, Universal Design activities should be integrated into the software de-velopment process. It is necessary to focus on diversity from the start and keep it up throughout the design process. Tasks and users are equally important. If you do not know what the service is, you will not know who needs it and when. Similarly, if you do not know what users think and do, you do not know what they need. It is widely recognized that a user centred development process with several iterations is suitable for developing ICT services.

An iterative development process is one that supports development of a system or service incrementally. The system or service is developed in several sections called iterations. The idea is that each iteration will deliver a working, although incomplete version of the system so that it can be reviewed and tested by stakeholders, including the service owner, customers and potential users. One usually starts with some key aspects of the system. The system functionality is expanded and adjusted according to refined and deeper understanding and changing requirements in every iteration. It is therefore important to make sure that Universal Design related information, such as relevant standards, results from user research, tests and evaluations, is frequently communicated and discussed within the development team. Revisions and new priorities must be communicated at appropriate points in time, at least at the beginning of each iteration cycle. It is inherent in this way of thinking that the requirements and their relative importance will change during the development process. Therefore one must consider how to handle such changing requirements, both from a technical perspective and from an organisational perspective. One change may affect several parts of a system. One must also consider who should be involved in the process of prioritizing new and changing requirements.

It is important to plan how to find and include people with disabilities and other differing capabilities in the design and development process. The process of recruiting for user involvement, investigation and user testing should begin early because this usually takes time. Organisations working for the rights and interests of people with disabilities are often helpful with passing on knowledge, information and contacts with potential test users.

STANDARDS AND GUIDELINES

There exist accessibility guidelines and standards for many ICT products and services, and these will provide a primary guide for ensuring accessibility (for example W3C 2005b, and ISO/TS 16071 2003).

There has been extensive work on understanding the barriers to, and the implementation of, ICT for physical disabilities, but much less work dealing with cognitive disability and appropriate user interface design. However Webaim gives some guidelines on this issue (Webaim 2007).

The American law, Section 508, effective June 21, 2001, requires Federal departments and agencies that develop, procure, maintain, or use electronic and information technology to ensure that these technologies are accessible for people with disabilities. Together with the law there are standards, resources and evaluation tools at the section 508 website[3]. For more guidance on standards see the chapter by Walter Mellors in this book.

USER RESEARCH

Common statements in user centred design are "know your user", and "if you try to design for all, you might not design for anybody, so therefore make sure that you at least design for somebody". The essence of these statements is that you have to do a thorough job of end user research. This is even more important when aiming at Universal Design.

User centred design often starts with gathering information about the end user population and then defining user groups. End user research can be done by selecting several techniques to complement and extend each other. For example examine who are the stake holders of the service, read

---

[3] http://www.section508.gov/index.cfm.

market research and surveys, use focus group interviews and contextual interviews, and observe potential users using similar products.

Often we narrow the user population too soon. For example, the potential users of a service announcing delays in train arrivals and departure will not only be travellers, but also people working in the railway organization and people having appointments with the traveller. Another example is that you cannot assume that all customers wanting to buy auto insurance can drive a car. For example a visually impaired person may very well want to compare auto insurance rates for a family member.

Having gathered a picture of the user population, it is often divided into sub groups that are seen as fairly homogenous (Shneiderman 1998). In Universal Design, however, you should look for the diverse characteristics of potential members of each subgroup, (e.g., with respect to gender; age; native language; physical and cognitive abilities). From the defined subgroups of the service you could create a set of user profiles. One way of making the process of describing the users manageable is to analyse and extend each sub group (or user profile) with respect to different impairments or situations such as in the table presented before.

DIFFERENT PERSPECTIVES

An ICT service is usually a complex system. In order to avoid undesirable mistakes and surprises it is wise to actively use different perspectives during the design process. Let the different stakeholders check the design. Vary your point of view by seeing the use situation from all the different user groups' perspectives, from the service provider's perspective etc.

When based on and combined with user research the use of "Personas" can be another powerful technique to bring in new perspectives and highlight diverse characteristics of users. It is also a method that is engaging and fun (Grudin

& Pruitt 2002). A persona is a hypothetical archetype of real users described in great detail and refined by their goals and needs, rather than just pure demographics (Lindgren et al. 2007). Personas should be created on the basis of the information gathered in the user research process. A set of personas should cover the different disabilities that might occur in the user group. The description of a persona should include the use environment and any assistive technology that the user needs. The use of personas in the methodology may bring up important aspects of individual differences, not only with respect to demographics, but also with respect to personalities, goals and abilities (ibid.). Their use tends to bring up more concrete design issues as opposed to a more generalized approach (e.g. using "average" user profiles). One can extend the different scenarios and narratives by using the personas. In order to get this method to work properly it is necessary for the development team to know the personas very well.

EVALUATION

In order to evaluate the service with regard to Universal Design, one should use different methods. As a first check it is wise to use accessibility tools[4]. For example there exist several web accessibility evaluation tools. These are software programs or online services that can help to determine whether a web site meets certain accessibility standards and guidelines.

The relationship between human computer interaction, usability and Universal Design in ICT is very close, and is beginning to get more attention (Petrie & Kheir 2007). Sometimes designers who are required to follow specific accessibility standards follow them strictly without truly understanding accessibility and usability issues. A well known example of this is the use of text alternatives to images on web pages. The accessibility rule is to provide a text alternative to images in order to make the page understandable for visually impaired people. Describing each decorative element

---

[4] See for example http://www.w3.org/WAI/ER/tools/ and http://www.smc.edu/disabledstudent/WebAccess/webaccess_eval.htm

on a web page however, only leads to information overload and poor usability for a visually impaired person. Trying to follow accessibility standards without seeing accessibility and usability in relationship may give ineffective and even unusable solutions. This is one of the reasons why user research and user testing is essential in Universal Design. The (ISO/TS 16071 2003) provides guidance on accessibility for human-computer interfaces. It clearly defines accessibility with reference to usability as:

The usability of a product, service, environment or facility by people with the widest range of capabilities.

Because of the close relation between usability and accessibility, methods of evaluating and testing accessibility should be extended by the evaluation of usability and vice versa. Examples of usability evaluation methods are heuristic evaluation and user tests.

Heuristic evaluation is a quick, cheap and easy technique for finding usability problems in a user-interface or product (Nielsen, Jakob 1993; Nielsen, Jacob 2005). Using a predefined set of rules or "heuristics", a small set of evaluators examines and judges the service. Heuristics typically look much like well-known high-level design principles. Selection of the specific heuristics or rules is important: often they must be adjusted to the particular application, product or service to be evaluated. One should make sure that the heuristics include accessibility rules and guidelines in addition to usability rules. Heuristic evaluation can be done by a single evaluator, but as different persons tend to find different problems, this is by no means optimal. According to Nielsen (1994) five evaluators will normally be sufficient to find 75 % of the usability problems in an application.

A heuristic evaluation will often lead to the discovery of more local problems, and more problems in total than a user test (Molich et al. 2004), but this may depend on the experience of those conducting the evaluation (ibid.). Because of this, and because it is difficult to determine the seriousness of the problems discovered, the method has had some criticism (Molich et al. 2004). However, usability tests have proven to be a good and cost effective method to discover unique and significant usability problems (Dumas & Redish 1999). The two methods can therefore be seen as complementary (ibid.).

A common method for user testing is the "Thinking aloud" method. This is described in several books on usability testing (Constantine & Lockwood 2000; Dumas & Redish 1999; Nielsen, Jakob 1993). The users are instructed to say out loud what they are doing, thinking and feeling while they use the ICT service or application.

As suggested above one should include the different types of disabilities (and situations if relevant) for each user group. This makes up a matrix that may grow quite large. Ideally one would need to test all these variants, but in the real world this might not be possible. In that case one should focus on getting a distribution encompassing diverse characteristics (gender, age, language, physical, and cognitive abilities). One option would be to include different types of disabilities in each usability test. As the development often goes through several iterations of usability testing, one can include participants with different characteristics in each round of testing. The user test can then be supplemented by going through the test scenarios with personas with other types of disabilities. This approach is more manageable, in terms of time and resources, than trying to fit participants representing all disability characteristics into one test. In any case, it is a good idea to include elderly in each user test, because they may have losses in certain cognitive, perceptual, and motor skills that can make using technology difficult. As the development and design team gets more experienced, it might draw upon earlier experience and concentrate on the aspects of a service that are new.

When doing user tests with people with disabilities it is important to consider the practicalities around this and the use of assistive technology. It is often effective to let users use their own equipment and assistive technology because it is usually personalised and it might be difficult to get the settings right with borrowed equipment. There is a risk that a user test with borrowed equipment would be disturbed by unfamiliar features and settings of the assistive technology. On the other hand, in a lab with standard equipment one would have more control of all settings and parameters. One would also often have easier access to tools supporting the user test, such as eye tracking, videos and logs. The practicalities should be discussed before and during the recruitment process.

SUMMARY

This chapter has presented some arguments for Universal Design in ICT services. It has endeavoured to show that designing for diversity and aiming at Universal Design, in addition to including people with disabilities, may lead to services that can be used in different environments and situations. The role of multimodality in Universal Design of ICTs has been discussed. A universally designed user interface should allow the users to select the most appropriate mode of interaction for their current needs, including any disabilities. The user interaction should depend upon the users' abilities, situation, preferences and devices, see Figure 1: Accommodating diversity in situations, devices and demographics.

Figure 1: Accommodating diversity in situations, devices and demographics

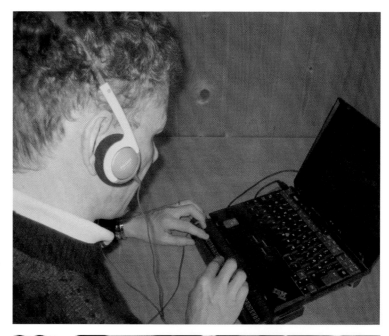

This chapter has also discussed the importance of planning with and integrating Universal Design activities in the development process. The following issues should be considered in the design of ICT services:

- Knowledge, attitude and commitment in the development organization. Educate the service and project owner, the management and the development team about Universal Design.

- Plan with iterations, user involvement and changing requirements. Universal Design activities must be integrated in the development process from the very beginning.

- Identify relevant standards and guidelines

- Perform user research

- Use different perspectives in the design process

- Evaluate and iterate

REFERENCES

Constantine, L. L. & Lockwood, L. A. D. (2000). Software for Use: A practical Guide to the Models and Methods of Usage Centered Design, Addison-Wesley. 579 p.

Dumas, J. S. & Redish, J. C. (1999). A practical guide to usability testing. Revised edition ed. Exeter, Intellect Books. 404 p.

Grudin, J. & Pruitt, J. (2002). Personas, Participatory Design and Product Development: An Infrastructure for Engagement. The Participatory Design Conference. 144–161 p.

ISO/TS 16071 (2003). Ergonomics of human-system interaction - Guidance on accessibility for human-computer interfaces. Technical specification. International Organisation for Standardisation. Switzerland, ISO.

ITU. (2007). Market Information and Statistics. International Telecommunication Union, ICT Statistics. Accessed 17 Dec. 2007, URL: http://www.itu.int/ITU-D/ict/statistics/ict/index.html.

Lindgren, A., Chen, F., Amdahl, P. & Chaikiat, P. (2007). Using Personas and Scenarios as an Interface Design Tool for Advanced Driver Assistance Systems. Universal Access in HCI, Part II, HCII 2007. Springer-Verlag Berlin Heidelberg. 460-469 p.

Molich, R., Ede, M. R., Kaasgaard, K. & Karyukin, B. (2004). Comparative usability evaluation. Behav. Inf. Tech., 23 (1): 65-74.

Mosner, E., Spiezle, C. & Emerman, J. (2003). The Convergence of the Aging Workforce And Accessible Technology, The implications for commerce, business and policy, Accessible Technology Group, Microsoft Corp.

NCD. (2001). The accessible future. Washington, USA, National Council on Disability.

Nielsen, J. (1993). Usability Engineering, AP Professional. 362 p.

Nielsen, J. (2005). Heuristic Evaluation. Accessed March 2007 URL: http://www.useit.com/papers/heuristic/.

Obrenovic, Z., Abascal, J. & Starcevic, D. (2007). Universal accessibility as a multimodal design issue. Commun. ACM, 50 (5): 83-88.

Perlman, G. (2002). Achieving Universal Usability by Designing for Change. IEEE Internet Computing, 6 (2): 46-55.

Petrie, H. & Kheir, O. (2007). The relationship between accessibility and usability of websites. Proceedings of the

SIGCHI conference on Human factors in computing systems, San Jose, California, USA. ACM Press.

Shneiderman, B. (1998). Designing the user interface. Strategies for Effective Human-Computer-Interaction. 3rd ed., Addison Wesley Longman, Inc.

Shneiderman, B. (2000). Universal Usability. Communications of the ACM, 43 (5): 84-91.

Statistics Canada & OECD, Desjardins, R., Murray, S., Clermont, Y. & Werquin, P. (2005). Learning a Living: First results of the adult literacy and life skills survey. OECD, Statistics Canada.

Vanderheiden, G. (2000). Fundamental principles and priority setting for universal usability. Proceedings of the 2000 conference on Universal Usability, Arlington, Virginia, United States. ACM Press.

W3C (2005a). Device Independence, Accessibility, and Multimodal Interaction. Accessed 1 November 2006, URL: http://www.w3.org/2005/04/di_mmi_wai.html.

W3C (2005b) Web Content Accessibility Guidelines (WCAG) Overview, version 1.1, ed. Henry, S L; Accessed 21 September 2007, URL: http://www.w3.org/WAI/intro/wcag.php.

WebAIM. (2007). Cognitive Disabilities, WebAIM is a non-profit organization within the Center for Persons with Disabilities at Utah State University, United States. Accessed 6 April 2007, URL: http://www.webaim.org/articles/cognitive/.

BJØRN HESTNES is Senior Research Scientist at Telenor Research & Innovation in Norway. He has over 25 years' experience of research work within real-time video communication. As a project leader for more than 20 user-centred projects, his work spans videotelephony for blind people, designing electronic classrooms, testing heterogeneous video communication, case studies in remote inspection, multi-site video communication and 3G video calls. He has a Master's degree in System Development from the University of Oslo.

PETER BROOKS is a British Chartered Psychologist specializing in user-centered interdisciplinary research on Information and Communication Technology (ICT). He has over 20 years of multinational experience spanning the main public and private research environments for Human Factors: in industry for ITT (in the UK) and Alcatel (in Germany); as a lecturer at Cranfield University (in the UK) and as a project manager for the SINTEF independent research institute (in Norway). Since 2003 he has focused on independent consultancy based in France, with clients including Telenor and the European Telecommunications Standards Institute.

SVEIN HEIESTAD is Chief Engineer at Telenor Research & Innovation. He has more than 25 years of research experience on how users experience videoconferencing situations and mobile video applications. He has participated in both national and multinational research, European Union projects and in ETSI (European Telecommunications Standards Institute) Specialist Task Forces.

USE OF MOBILE VIDEO TELEPHONY BY BLIND PEOPLE: INCREASING INDEPENDENCE AND SPONTANEITY FOR DAY-TO-DAY LIFE

Bjørn Hestnes, Peter Brooks and Svein Heiestad

INTRODUCTION

Videotelephony for blind persons may sound a contradiction in terms. However, using two-way audio and one-way video from a blind or visually impaired person to a service operator, a new and important communication service may have been born. With the help of persons who can see and act as guides, visually impaired persons could obtain information on what is present in their surroundings. The videophone could be either a stationary or mobile device. This chapter is concerned with empirical tests of a mobile service concept.

The terminal for the visually impaired person could be a 3G (third-generation mobile) phone, of which there are many candidates on the market such as the Nokia 6680 (Figure 1 right). It could also be a wearable computer such as the Visi-Wear terminal (Figure 1 left). The operator's terminal could either consist of a monitor for video plus a desktop computer for other information, or a single computer that also includes a video window.

The application of videotelephony to see details of a remote environment may be referred to as "remote inspection" (Hestnes et al., 2001a). Case studies of remote inspection tested in the offshore oil business and road construction industry have found that still images can not support remote inspection i.e. moving images such as video are essential (Hestnes et al., 2001b). The network QoS (Quality of Service) therefore became critical with this need for video information.

The effects of changes in QoS parameters on user behaviour have mainly been studied for face-to-face applications of videotelephony rather than remote inspection (e.g., O'Malley et al. 2003). However, O'Malley et al. (2003) report provisional results for a remote inspection task involving communication of procedural skill. It was concluded that delay did not affect task performance whereas packet loss may have an effect. Different remote inspection tasks are likely to require different critical-value QoS parameters. For example, for viewing a moving scene the frame-rate could become more critical, whilst for viewing image detail the screen resolution may become important.

Figure 1 Left:VisiWear's wearable computer. Right: Nokia's mobile (video)phone 6680.

Whilst no other work appears to have applied mobile videotelephony to the needs of blind people, the potential of mobile videotelephony for deaf people has been studied in terms of support for sign language and lip reading (Frowein et al. 2001; Post & Telestyrelsen 2005). Work on wearable computers and mobile audio devices for blind and visually impaired people has primarily focused on assisting navigation. For example, Lok (2004) describes a prototype with a GPS sensor which works in conjunction with a head-tracking sensor on headphones to track the wearer's location and direction. The wearable computer plays beeps over the headphones, and the user moves toward the apparent source of the sound. This application is therefore intended for following a pre-programmed route, whereas real-time communication with a remote service operator would enable spontaneous aid for navigation. The combination of providing GPS information to a service centre with mobile audio contact with a visually-impaired person has been investigated (Adams-Spink, 2007). However, using a videophone could enable assistance in many more situations where visual information is important.

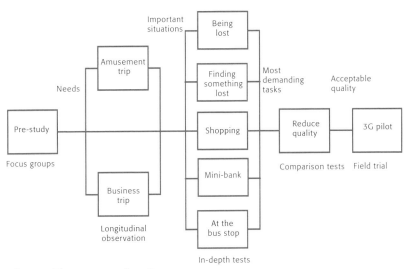

Figure 2. The sequence of studies

Early questions concerning the potential application of mobile videotelephony for visually impaired persons involve the relevance of the service concept for intended users, their most likely usage situations and the acceptable technical quality level given foreseeable terminals and networks. This chapter therefore addresses these questions by describing a sequence of studies (Figure 2):

- Focus group studies performed to pre-test the service concept and to identify initial user and technical require-ments

- Longitudinal studies of leisure- and business use to identify specific needs
- User tests performed in five identified important situations
- Technical quality comparison tests performed on the most demanding sub-tasks identified in the user tests
- A field trial with off-the-shelf 3G mobile handsets.

FOCUS GROUP STUDY OF SERVICE CONCEPT

The focus group studies involved 19 participants in 6 groups of up to 4 people. All participants were either totally blind or severely visually impaired (Lunde et al., 2001). The study found enthusiasm for the service concept and two categories of situations were identified for potential use of the service:

- At home or at work, where users might obtain assistance for such tasks as checking their post, determining if their clothes are clean and that colours match.
- "Anywhere" for such tasks as finding the way to a shop, identifying items in a shop and receiving descriptions of surroundings for leisure and cultural benefit (e.g. outdoor landscapes).

LONGITUDINAL OBSERVATION STUDIES OF LEISURE AND BUSINESS TRAVEL

A specially designed wearable computer was used. The whole unit was attached to a belt. The wearable computer had WLAN (Wireless Local Area Network) connection to transmit CIF-information (Common Intermediate Format, 352x288 pixels) with a frame rate of 25 fps (frames per second) from a handheld camera. The audio system had telephone quality sound in the frequency range of 300-3400 kHz. The appearance of the videophone when worn by a person is shown in Figure 3 left.

The service centre operator had a laptop computer with the screen displaying the video image from the test person. A second map window provided an additional option to determine the location of the user (Figure 3 centre).

In order to carry out a test with best quality video (25 fps and 352x288 pixels) the service centre operator was not in a remote location for this trial, as no network was available with the necessary bandwidth and quality for all tests. The operator stayed in the location of the videophone user and test team to use a peer-to-peer Local Area Network (LAN). The service operator was typically 20-50 meters (22-55 yards) away from the test participant. The operator's laptop computer was supported by shoulder straps at all times and a tripod if desired when stationary (Figure 3 right).

Two observational studies involved two different blind persons who undertook significant activities with the mobile video call service that they would not otherwise perform without co-present human support. In both cases the theme was 'a trip': For one blind person this was a three-day leisure-oriented trip using an international ferry, train and hotel (Hestnes et al., 2003). For the other blind person it was a local work-oriented trip to the premises of a client that involved urban travel by underground train and walking.

Whenever the two study participants decided to use the mobile video call service, the call achieved its aim. The service centre operator reported that every task initiated was solved properly and that he was able to cope with an image from a camera that was held in all positions (including upside down) and did not need to ask the visually impaired participant to rotate the camera.

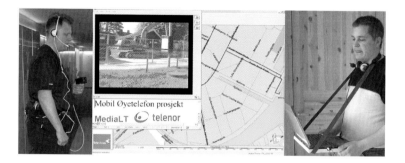

Figure 3. Left: Test person with terminal; middle: Service centre operator's view of monitor; right: Service centre operator with test terminal.

There were three main situations when the video call was used:

- *To verify* information or objects when found (after finding something either independently or with video call help)
- *To search* for information or objects
- *To observe* a situation, object or environment.

		Purpose of call		
		Verify	Search	Observe
Spontaneity of call	Spontaneous	"Wasn't my room number 1012? I have to check."	"So now I have arrived here, but where is the exit?"	"Describe how my child is enjoying herself"
	Planned	No example identified.	"I've arrived as planned by bus, please direct me to the underground station"	"In about two hours, I will be up at the top and want to experience the view".

Table 1. Classification of mobile video call service usage

Sometimes the test person used the video call in a planned way and sometimes spontaneously. This led to classification of mobile video call service use on the basis of 'Purpose of the call' and 'Spontaneity of call' as illustrated in Table 1. As can be seen in Table 1, for this case study not all possible types of use from the derived classification were observed.

On the basis of both case studies it was concluded that the video call worked well where sighted people would not experience any major problems in interacting with their environment. Calls to the service operator took longer in situations when sighted people would probably also experience problems (e.g. poor hotel lift exit design, poor shop display) or can expect to experience initial problems (e.g. first time use of an automatic cash dispenser). However, even in these particularly demanding situations the two study participants were successful.

USER TESTS OF KEY SITUATIONS

The aims of the in-depth user tests were to:

- examine user satisfaction and task effectiveness when using a video call for key situations identified in the focus groups and observational studies
- identify particularly demanding tasks within the situations where Quality of Service (QoS) may be a critical factor and subject for further study.

The five most relevant situations identified for video call use are summarised in Table 2. Each situation is classified on the basis of the main types of tasks that were expected to take place in that situation, using the classification scheme in Table 1. Each usage situation was tested by 10 persons who were blind or severely visually impaired.

The same test equipment was used as in the two longitudinal observational studies. The same service-centre operator who participated in the 'leisure trip' observational study acted as the remote helper. A test session with each participant involved the use of the mobile videophone for each of the five situations in sequence. A typical test session took from two to four hours.

#	Name	Description	Classification
1.	Mini-bank	Withdraw money from a cash-dispenser	Search & Verify
2.	Shopping	Select food item(s) within a single shop	Search, Verify & Observe
3.	At a bus stop	Identify correct bus as it arrives at bus stop	Search, Verify & Observe
4.	Finding something lost on the ground	Retrieve a dropped item	Search & Verify
5.	Being lost	Walk to a familiar or safe location	Search & Observe

Table 2. The five situations tested

The mobile videophone service had very high effectiveness as measured by successful task completion (100 % in four situations) and was rated very highly in terms of satisfaction (mean overall rating = 8 out of 9). The lowest rated situation was where the mobile videophone service was the least effective, but this situation (Item lost) still obtained a mean satisfaction score of 6 (out of 9) and an 80 % (8/10) success rate.

TESTS OF TECHNICAL QUALITY REDUCTION

High quality video was used in the studies described above in order to explore many situations where a future service may be of good utility. Some situations of mobile videophone use may not be feasible if the technical quality of the service is lower. During the in-depth tests the service centre operator was asked to identify sub-tasks where the demand on the technology appeared particularly high. The service operator assessed the Shopping situation to be the most demanding, because it was necessary to find the right area of food while the users where walking and to read small text on an article or a label. Therefore two key areas were identified for testing: where there is a high demand on movement and where there is a high demand on screen resolution. For screen resolution three quality levels were tested: CIF (Common Intermediate Format with 352x288 pixels); QCIF (Quarter CIF with 176x144 pixels); SQCIF (Sub QCIF with 117x83 pixels). For transmitting movements four levels of frame rate were used: 2-3 fps; 5-6 fps; 10-15 fps; 25 fps.

For these tests the service operator who had been the remote helper for the in-depth tests was the person who was required to judge what was visible on the service screen. Although the results are only based on qualitative judgements by one person, they are considered to have good validity as this person was the professional service centre operator who participated in the 50 user tests and because the tests were focused on the two most challenging situations for video quality that this operator had identified. However, further work with a larger sample size is recommended in order to test if these results can be replicated.

The tables of results for the movement tests (Table 3) distinguish three categories of legibility: Unreadable, Sometimes readable; and Acceptable.

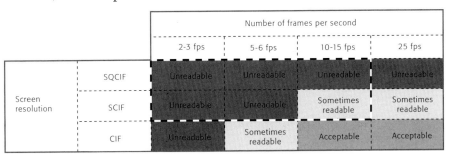

		Number of frames per second			
		2-3 fps	5-6 fps	10-15 fps	25 fps
Screen resolution	SQCIF	Unreadable	Unreadable	Unreadable	Unreadable
	SCIF	Unreadable	Unreadable	Sometimes readable	Sometimes readable
	CIF	Unreadable	Sometimes readable	Acceptable	Acceptable

Table 3 Acceptability for movement and screen.
Key: ⌐ ¬ *Area of technical quality in which 3G operates*

It is therefore recommended that the operator should receive at least CIF and 10 fps quality information for the video window. This advice is based on the use of a good camera with good auto-iris and auto-focus with macro-capability.

These results show that the quality areas in which 3G is operating are the 'Unreadable' and 'Sometimes readable' categories (illustrated in Table 3). Thus 3G will not be acceptable for all situations.

3G FIELD TRIAL

Whereas it is concluded in the previous section that a mobile video call service should have at least the video quality of CIF with 10 frames per second, the videotelephony service on 3G has lower quality (see Table 3). The 3G video resolution has between 11-25% of the number of pixels giving SQCIF or QCIF quality. Also the number of frames is usually not constant and typically varies between 5-15 fps. It was therefore considered important to test a real but potentially non-ideal application of available technology.

The 3G field trial took place in Norway with nine visually impaired persons from August to December 2005. At that time the only network available was Telenor's UMTS network which was half-way through its build-out period. The Nokia 6680 handset was chosen for the trial, along with the TALK client which synthesises text on the screen into audio.

Originally ten persons were recruited, with a 50/50 gender split and a deliberate variation in age (mean = 41 years, standard deviation = 11, youngest = 25, eldest = 62). Eight of these people were totally blind and two were severely visually impaired. Additional participants were the service providers of a text-telephony service centre. A total of 20 handsets were sponsored, so that each trial participant could keep one handset for themselves and give a second to another person that would be their helper when called instead of the service centre. At an early stage one visually impaired person decided not to participate.

The visually impaired participants were asked to use their handset for videotelephony as and when they decided. They attended an initial start-up meeting to receive their two handsets, receive a brief overview of the 3G network and learn how to make a vidotelephony call and use the TALKS client. A few days later the service centre called the visually impaired participants to make first contact and to try out the service.

Semi-structured questionnaires recorded the visually impaired participants' expectations for the service before use. Further questionnaires were sent out mid-way through the trial and at the end, primarily to measure frequency and purpose of use.

Each visually impaired participant was interviewed at least once during the trial period and was free to contact a dedicated person in the research team at any time for support.

After 5 months the 3G handset was being used for video calls on average 3 times per week. The majority of calls were made to the participant's personal helper, with an average of less than 1 call (0.8) per week to the service centre.

All of the participants stated that they intend to continue to use the mobile video call service after the trial. Six of the nine participants expected the frequency of use to be about the same whilst one person expected to use it more and two participants expected frequency of use to decrease.

The general user goals for which 3G videotelephony was applied are summarised in Table 4. As these were responses to an open question, these expressions represent what occurred to the participants. Table 5 summarises the usage situations that were reported by applying the distinction between "Search", "Verify" and "Observe" tasks as in Table 1.

When asked directly whether a mobile video call service had helped make their lives simpler, 6 of the nine participants responded 'Yes'. From an analysis of their usage situations and anecdotes, this very positive outcome would seem to be

because mobile videotelephony can provide increased independence, spontaneity, safety and efficiency in day-to-day life.

User goal	Example statement	Number of participants (N=9) stating goal
Greater freedom & independency	"I can move in new areas"	7
Spontaneity	"I can get help at any time"	5
Improved safety	"I know I have someone to ask"	3
Efficiency	"Tasks get done quicker"	2

Table 4. Main communication goals

User task	Examples
Search	For lost things (e.g., item dropped on the ground, a guide dog that does not return)
	For locations in buildings (e.g., gate, toilet, food at an airport)
	Item sorting (e.g. post, audio books, money)
	Entrance to a house
Verify	Correct selection (e.g., temperature on the cooker, programme on washing machine)
	Colour matching of clothes
	Presence/absence of item (e.g., injury to a child, symptoms of illness)
Observe	Description of the environment or a person
	Description of an event
	Read a computer screen, signs, doctor's prescription, medicine box, food packaging, recipes

Table 5. Classification of usage

The main problem reported by the participants was the lack
of coverage of the 3G network. The quality of the video was
criticised for a number of reasons:

- unsuitable for details in the environment when the hanset is moved
- difficult for small items, such as reading some characters in text
- unsuitable in poor light conditions (relative darkness or with counter-light such when as the sun is in the picture).

During the trial the cost of using the call centre was fixed at €3 per call. This was considered too much.

Technical support from the researchers was requested approximately twice a month. This was mainly about problems with network coverage, turning on the video and operating the TALKS programme. Over the 5 month period two handsets developed a fault.

OVERALL CONCLUSIONS

The 3G study confirmed a real value in using mobile videotelephony for assisting the day-to-day life of visually impaired people, as previously concluded for shorter-term tests with a high quality prototype system.

The different studies were consistent in showing that the main uses of a mobile videophone for this user group are to Search, Verify and Observe. Therefore the mobile system should be able to support these three tasks and a 3G handset operating on a UMTS network was found capable of achieving the main goals of the nine participants who completed the trial. This was with a system of lower quality than concluded necessary for achieving the most demanding tasks in the earlier quality comparison test. The participants found the 3G system useful despite the lower quality; but, as expected, for viewing the environment and for reading small text it was inadequate.

These test results represent potentially useful data for service and systems developers and have been used to develop guide-lines for industry on user quality of experience (Brooks et al., 2006; ETSI, 2007).

If a network to support 3G handsets is in place, it can be expected that people who are visually impaired will want to use it. However, call price is an issue and fear of incurring financial cost can be expected to inhibit use. The series of studies described indicate that typical use of a mobile video call service would be fairly frequent, short calls. Therefore a pricing model that does not deter this could result in good use of mobile videotelephony by persons who are visually impaired.

REFERENCES

Adams-Spink, G. (2007). "GPS navigation plan to help blind" http://news.bbc.co.uk/1/hi/technology/6458005.stm

(Brooks et al., 2006) Brooks, P., Hestnes, B., Heiestad, S., Aaby, C. (2006). "Communicating Quality of Experience data for the development of multimedia services". Proceedings of the 20th International Symposium on Human Factors in Telecommunication, Sophia Antipolis, France, March 21-23 2006, (available from http://www.hft.org/HFT06/HFT_06_programme.htm).

(ETSI 2006) ETSI EG 202 534 "Human Factors (HF); Guidelines for real-time person-to-person communication services".

(Frowein et al. 2001) Frowein, H., Kamphuis, H., Rikken, E. (2001). Sign language interpretation via mobile videotelephony. Proceedings of the 18th International Symposium on Human Factors in Telecommunication, Bergen, Norway 5-7, 2001, pp. 191-196.

(Hestnes el al., 2001a) Hestnes, B., Heiestad, S., Brooks, P.,

Drageset, L. (2001). Real situations of wearable computers used for video conferencing - and implications for terminal and network design. Proceedings of the Fifth International Symposium on Wearable Computers (pp. 85-93), Zürich, 8-9 October 2001. IEEE Computer Society, USA

(Hestnes el al., 2001b) Hestnes, B., Heiestad, S., Brooks, P. (2001). Mobile videoconferencing (remote inspection) used in maintenance and operation – results from two case studies. Kjeller, Telenor R&D (FOU report R15/2001).

(Hestnes et al., 2003) (Hestnes 2003) Hestnes, B., Brooks, P., Heiestad, S., Tollefsen, M. (2003). "Eye-phone" - case study results from the application of videotelephony for blind people.. Proceedings of the 19th International Symposium on Human Factors in Telecommunication, Berlin, Germany, December 1-4 2003, pp. 135-142.

(Lok, 2004) Lok, C. (2004) Wireless for the Disabled. Technology Review (01/04) Vol. 106 (10), p 64.

(Lunde et al., 2001) Lunde, M., Tollefsen, M., Hestnes, B., (2001). Øyetelefonen-Et forprosjekt i regi av Norges Forskningsråd/IT Funk. (Available from Norges Forskningsråd, Norway).

(O'Malley et al. 2003) O'Malley, C. , Brundell, P., McFadzean, J., Lonsdale, P., Schliemann, T. et al. (2003) Results of Laboratory Experiments of Communication Media. IST Project 1999-11577. Eye-2-Eye: Fitness-for-purpose of Person-Person Communication Technologies, CEC Deliverable IST11577/ UON/SOP/DS/Pub/003/b1, December 2002.

(Post & Telestyrelsen 2005) Mobile video communications for people who are deaf: Report on trial operations with broadband for people with disability. Swedish National Post and Telecom Agency Report No. PTS-ER-2005:14.

INDEX

I

Inclusive design 5, 13, 131, 134, 177, 182, 183, 194, 247
    process 136

Information and Communication Technology (ICT) 5, 236, 245, 269

Iterations 255
    for developing ICT services 256

N

New markets 6, 178

P

Principles
    of universal design 11, 33, 86, 159, 183

Product design
    engineering 180

R

Requirements
    user 70, 224, 225, 230

S

Service design 145

Sustainability 7, 17, 160
    social 7, 23

Stigmatizing 182, 183

U

Universal design 4-7, 55
    center for 29, 32
    concepts behind 5
    evaluation (EDU) 33, 34, 39, 43
    pedagogic method 15
    performance criteria 33-35
    process 42
    why in ICT 247, 260

Usability 4, 57, 58, 145
    testing 230, 254, 261
    triangle 169
    universal 247

Use
    contexts 252, 254
    easy to 165, 219

User
    -centered design 2, 17
    experience 195, 205
    friendly 142, 157, 193
    trials 148